Yun Ko-eun was born in Seoul in 1980. Her short story 'Piercing' won the Daesan Literary Award for College Students the year she graduated from university. She received the 2008 Hankyoreh Literature Award for her novel *The Zero G Syndrome*, in 2011 her short story 'The Hippocampus, Fly' won the Lee Hyo-seok Literary Award and in 2015 her short story collection *Aloha* won the Kim Yong-ik Novel Prize.

Praise for *The Disaster Tourist*

'A gripping literary thriller about disaster, adventure and a crisis of conscience that will resonate with any traveller' **Jennifer Croft**, author of *Homesick* and winner of the Man Booker International Prize for her translation of Olga Tokarczuk's *Flights*

'A labyrinth of catastrophes and cataclysms, *The Disaster Tourist* is a precisely penned novel that lays bare the human condition. Mysterious, evocative and rich' **Sarah Rose Etter**, author of *The Book of X*

'Excellent ... a plain rendering of the extraordinary' *Irish Times*

'An exciting up-and-coming writer tackling gender ... these themes aren't unique to South Korea, but [are] ones that resonate with women globally' **Katie Goh**, *i-D*

'A mordantly witty novel that touches on everything from the rise of "dark tourism" to sexual predators in the office to climate change ... a highly literary ultra-incisive thriller' **Refinery29**

'Brings too close to home ... believe are far away, sep... *Books*

The Disaster Tourist

Yun Ko-eun

Translated by Lizzie Buehler

This paperback edition published in 2021

First published in Great Britain in 2020 by
Serpent's Tail
an imprint of Profile Books Ltd
29 Cloth Fair
London EC1A 7JQ
www.serpentstail.com

Copyright © Yun Ko-eun, 2020

English translation copyright © Lizzie Buehler, 2020

This book is published with the support of
the Literature Translation Institute of Korea (LTI Korea)

3 5 7 9 10 8 6 4 2

Typeset in Tramuntana Text by MacGuru Ltd
Designed by Nicky Barneby @ Barneby Ltd

Printed and bound in Great Britain by CPI Group (UK) Ltd, Croydon, CR0 4YY

A CIP catalogue record for this book is available from the British Library.

ISBN 978 1 78816 315 6
eISBN 978 1 78283 585 1

The
Disaster
Tourist

1

Jungle

–

Northbound: High atmospheric pressure, cherry blossoms, news of deaths
Southbound: Dust clouds, strikes, debris

NEWS OF THE DEATHS MOVED FAST that week. Word was spreading quickly, but it wouldn't be long before people lost interest. By the time funeral proceedings began, the public would have already forgotten the deceased.

A tsunami had hit Jinhae, in the province of Kyeongnam. Jinhae was where cherry blossoms first bloomed in early spring. When it happened, on an otherwise typical afternoon, life in the city had stopped. In an instant, everything was underwater: tourists beholding the flowers, pedestrians meandering about, buildings that had been warmed by the sun, and street lamps on the edge of the beach.

Yona went down to Jinhae on Friday evening.

Jungle – the travel company where she worked as a programming coordinator – didn't currently offer any travel packages to visit the post-tsunami rubble, but it would soon. After arriving, Yona's first tasks were to hand over donations and dispatch volunteers. She spent the weekend giving out money – ten-thousand-won contributions from nearly a thousand Jungle employees – expressing her condolences and assessing the situation. Jungle divided disasters into thirty-three distinct categories, including volcano eruptions, earthquakes, war, drought, typhoons and tsunamis, with 152 available packages. For the city of Jinhae, Yona planned to create an itinerary that combined viewing the aftermath of the tsunami with volunteer work.

Yona's return to Seoul took longer than the trek down south. As Korea marched into spring, cherry blossoms were blanketing the country. The flowers had already bloomed in Jinhae, and during Yona's weekend away from home, northern blossoms began to bud as well. Once she was back in Seoul, Yona turned on her TV. After the south coast tsunami, the news broadcast not only typical weather forecasts and programmes about the flowers' arrival, but also information about where the ocean currents would take the tsunami wreckage now trapped in their waters. The trash consisted of artefacts of daily life stolen by nature, mostly pieces of plastic and forgettable knick-knacks not yet decomposed. Soon to be forgotten by their former owners, they were destined to swirl about the sea for decades. The debris flowed south along the currents, bobbing atop ever-moving waves.

Predictions about the trash's future path varied. Some said it would flow into the garbage island in the Pacific Ocean, the one that was seven times the size of the Korean Peninsula. Others guessed that within the next two years it would end up along the coast of Chile. Some people even estimated where the trash would be ten years from now. Most citizens just hoped that they wouldn't cross paths with the tsunami's remains. They wanted to shield themselves from disaster, to hide from risk.

However, one segment of Korean society differed from the risk-averse majority. These voyagers carried survival kits, generators and tents as they searched out disaster zones worthy of exploration. They were the kind of people who would relish the chance to weather the open sea in search of the mythical island of trash. Jungle was the travel company for such adventurers.

Yona had once dreamed of going on treacherous journeys. The first place she'd ever travelled to was Nagasaki, her trip inspired by a single sentence in a guidebook: 'The city is home to statues commemorating citizens who lost their lives in the atomic bomb explosion, as well as those who passed away in local storms.' The guidebook mapped the location of the Nagasaki statues, but as she read, Yona had realised she didn't care where the statues were. Instead, she'd begun to wonder what exactly went missing when a person lost his or her life, and if the lost life was ever

3

found elsewhere. Yona was always wondering about this kind of unknown information – like where rocks that fell off the side of a mountain ended up. And what about the scales removed from a filleted fish, or unwanted potato sprouts, or even bullets?

Yona had worked at Jungle for over ten years, surveying disaster zones and moulding them into travel destinations. As a child, she hadn't imagined doing work like this, but she was skilled at quantifying the unquantifiable. The frequency and strength of disasters, and the resulting damage to humans and property, transformed into colourful graphs now spread out on Yona's desk. Next to the graphs lay a world map and a Korean map, place names marked with notations to indicate which disasters had occurred there. To Yona, certain places were now interchangeable with disaster. New Orleans made her think about the remaining traces of Hurricane Katrina. In New Zealand, it was the earthquake that had shaken the city of Christchurch into rubble. Near Chernobyl, the ghost towns that emerged after the region was exposed to radiation, along with the Red Forest created by the fallout. In Brazil, the favelas, and in Sri Lanka, Japan and Phuket – like in Jinhae – the damage wreaked by tsunamis. Ultimately, no city could ever completely evade catastrophe. Disaster lay dormant in every corner, like depression. You never knew when it might spring into terrible action, but if you were lucky, it could remain hidden for a lifetime.

Every year, the world experienced on average 900 earthquakes that measured higher than 5.0 on the

Richter scale, and 300 volcanoes – large and small – exploded across all seven continents. These facts were as quotidian to Yona as the changing colours of a traffic light. Only last year, almost 200,000 people had died in natural disasters. With an average of 100,000 annual deaths over the past ten years, calamity was growing more powerful and periodic. And while technological innovations prevented more and more catastrophe, new and wilier disasters popped up as well. Learning about misfortune was what Yona did. Because calamity was her job, it had a tendency to occupy her mind even during her off-hours. Working at Jungle was all encompassing.

'It's the customer service line,' Yona's subordinate said as he handed her the phone.

Now Yona would repeat phrases she'd said a thousand times, like an android on autopilot. 'Ma'am, if you cancel, you'll incur a service fee,' or 'Sir, this is specified in the contract.' Strictly speaking, this wasn't Yona's responsibility, but she had already fielded several customer complaints today. The calls were coming in at the most inopportune moment.

'I'm sorry, sir,' she said calmly into the phone, 'but refunds are not possible.'

Customers always responded to this sentence in the same way.

'But there are still three months left until the trip,' replied the voice on the other end. 'Why would there be a one hundred per cent penalty for cancellation? I'm cancelling because my child is sick. Are you really saying that there's no chance of a refund? Actually, why is it that none of your trips allow for cancellation?'

'Cancellations are possible, sir,' Yona said, 'but we cannot refund deposits already paid in full.'

'Cancellations are possible, but refunds aren't? Is it always like this? That means I should have only paid part of the deposit at first. If this is how you're going to be, I'll have to file a complaint with the Consumer Protection Bureau.'

'Would you like me to transfer you to them now?' Yona asked. 'I'm sorry to say, they won't be of any help. Our contract clearly stipulated from the beginning that your trip cannot be refunded, regardless of the date of cancellation. You signed the contract, sir. Since you've already paid the deposit, you received a large discount, so buying early wasn't a bad idea. If you still decide to go on the trip, rest assured that you received the best possible price. People signing up now are being charged thirty-five per cent more, even if they pay the reservation deposit up front.'

'Look.'

The customer's voice had grown cold.

'I told you that my child is sick. He's in the hospital. In a situation like this, can't you be a decent person and let me cancel?'

'If you'd like, we can cancel your order,' Yona said.

'But a refund isn't possible, right?' the man asked.

'That is correct, sir.'

'What is your name?'

'Sir—'

'I asked you what your name is! I'm done with all this crap. Tell me your name.'

'Yona Ko.'

With that, the man hung up. He was angry, and so was Yona. Most of the time, customers were more forgiving of higher-ranking employees, which was why customer service passed calls up to programming coordinators. On a day like today, though, when Yona was inundated with work, she didn't have time to be bothered by distractions. Jungle didn't want her to waste her efforts with disgruntled customers, either. Yona was one of the brains of the company, not its lips.

She wondered if her recent role change at Jungle might indicate that she was the target of a 'yellow card'. She had known about the company's preferred form of discipline since being hired. A yellow card was less a warning than a siren, signalling a growing and irreparable fissure. Once you'd received one, as long as the moon didn't fall out of the sky, you could do nothing to stop the already-widening fracture. Yona wondered if she might get an actual yellow slip of paper, by mail or email or even courier, but she knew better: that wasn't how it worked. Yellow cards showed themselves in a discreet manner, but were unmistakable, so that the recipient could appreciate the crisis that had befallen his or her career.

Two divergent paths faced the yellow card recipient: work as diligently as possible in a newly hostile office environment, or fight back with all of one's being. Yona had heard of someone who'd risen back to his original position, five years after a swift fall from grace. In the meantime, that person's assistant had become his boss. Even after returning to his original job, the man worked for only a brief period of time before quitting. His health was poor. Quite possibly, the shock of the yellow card and five years of tumult had caused a tumour in his brain. Yona didn't know him personally, but the story circulated through the office. Supposedly, the subject was the former head of the team one room over.

Recently, whenever Yona went into work, she'd felt like a dandelion seed that had somehow drifted into a building. The chair she sat in each morning was definitely hers, but for some reason, sitting in it was awkward, like this was the first time she'd ever touched the piece of furniture. She grew uncomfortable whenever she saw the new hires striding up and down the hallways, like giants already in control of the place. When Yona voiced her discomfort to a few close co-workers in the bathroom, they said that her complaints were baseless. As soon as Yona opened her mouth, their casual conversation – light as the paper towels they were throwing into the bin – took on a heaviness, and Yona's co-workers looked at her with very serious faces.

'Is something going on?' one friend asked.

Yona figured that she was making the situation worse by bringing it up, so she quickly washed her hands and tried to forget her unease. But the truth was, several days earlier there *had* been an uncomfortable incident. She'd shown up for a meeting on time, but when she arrived, no one was in the room. A wide-eyed junior staff member had approached Yona from the hallway.

'Isn't there a meeting?' Yona asked, confused, as she stepped out of the conference suite.

The man replied with a wink. 'Today's a foul.'

'A foul?' she asked.

'That's what they told me,' he said.

Foul? Was this some sort of new jargon? An abbreviation? A kind of slang? As Yona racked her brains, she remembered hearing a similar sentence a few days ago, in the department next to her own: 'It's because of a foul.'

'Okay,' she replied in a fluster, losing the chance to ask, 'But what's a foul?' Yona figured that she didn't have to determine the meaning of the word; she just needed to understand the situations in which it was used. But she didn't have any idea what those situations were. Of course, she could have just asked someone, but she felt uneasy letting people know that she didn't know what 'foul' meant.

The co-worker hurried away, and Yona stared blankly at the empty conference room before stepping into the lift. After meetings, employees would crowd into the bathroom or smoking area to relieve built-up tension, but today, even without such social exertion, Yona was too exhausted to do anything but rush back to her desk. As Yona boarded the lift; so did Kim – another co-worker. Once the doors closed, he spoke.

'Johnson is asking me to send my greetings to you,' Kim told Yona.

'Who?' Yona asked.

'Johnson. My Johnson.'

Kim pointed to his crotch. The lift was descending from the twenty-first to the third floor, and Kim and Yona were the only two people inside. Without even giving her a moment to be surprised, Kim grabbed at Yona's bottom. The action wasn't a mistake, it was deliberate: a brazen gesture that suggested Kim didn't care if he was caught.

'Are you older than I thought?' he taunted her. 'Why didn't you understand what I said?'

Yona turned her body as casually as she could to avoid eye contact with Kim. Now he was pushing his hand into her blouse. Yona's chest pounded furiously, although not because she was seeing the unsavoury side of Kim for the first time. Nor was it because her *boss* was sexually assaulting her. No: according to what Yona knew, Kim only targeted has-beens – employees who'd been given a yellow card, or who were about to receive one. She was horrified to think that her rejection of his advances might be the grounds for a yellow card.

Yona stepped aside, fearful of the CCTV on the wall behind her. She tried to stand still like nothing was happening. She didn't want the episode to be discovered; the CCTV recorded tirelessly, twenty-four hours a day. Additionally, Yona wasn't sure when the lift was going to open its door, revealing her and Kim to colleagues waiting on another floor. Kim was harassing her so shamelessly, he was almost asking for his actions to be made public. His touch felt extremely impersonal somehow: he didn't speak to Yona as he molested her. The doors to the lift lurched open and two people entered. By then, Kim's hand had already moved from Yona's chest back into his pocket. He said something in a low voice that the others may or may not have heard.

'You should pay a bit more attention to words,' he warned Yona. 'Not knowing the language of this day and age, that's like going around wearing a sign that says, "I don't care if I get left behind!"'

When Kim got off, the other riders in the lift sneaked glances at Yona. After that day, Kim slipped his cold hands inside Yona's skirt two more times. The important thing wasn't the temperature of his hand, it was the hand itself, but she hated the clamminess so much that just thinking about it gave her goosebumps. Kim had been Yona's immediate supervisor for the past ten years, and he kept her on board every time there were changes in personnel. He was a competent boss. Or to be more accurate, he wasn't a competent boss but a competent underling, and thanks to that he could maintain the facade of proficiency. Kim's employee performance rating was exactly fifty per cent, and his likes and dislikes were clear. He shook people he didn't approve of until they broke. Yona was frightened by the thought of others learning that she had become Kim's newest target. If his sexual offences remained covert, she was inclined to bear the discomfort. Yona thought about her complacency and then shook her head. No, what made her most uncomfortable right now was that she'd tolerated his actions three times without doing anything. She felt like she was somehow cooperating. But victims would understand her hesitation to act, she thought.

It was a warm spring. The first thing that came to mind when Yona thought of the season wasn't flowers or the budding leaves, but sweat. When she had visited the tsunami aftermath in Jinhae, sweat dripped down her neck the entire weekend. As soon as spring turned to summer, Kim called Yona into his office.

'You've committed a foul,' he said. 'I'm going to have to remove you from the team's current project. Why don't you focus on the maintenance of existing packages for now?'

The work Yona was assigned that afternoon would normally have been given to an intern.

'Shall we have a company dinner tomorrow, Manager Ko?' asked Kim the next day, using Yona's more formal title. He didn't really want her opinion and didn't wait for her response before going on. 'Everyone is busy, but that's exactly why we need to relax for a few hours. Let's not get *samgyeopsal* this time – let's try something a bit more special. Go ask everyone what they want to eat.'

Because of Kim and his love for documents, Yona's team ran out of A4 paper much faster than other teams. Recently, they'd been using up paper so quickly that they had to print everything double-sided. Yona asked her colleagues for their opinions about the dinner menu, and she typed up the results on a page that she printed out and brought to Kim.

The document and the information it contained dissipated into irrelevance as soon as Kim brashly said, 'Actually let's just eat *samgyeopsal*.'

Yona spent the next several days performing similar tasks. If she wasn't told to man the phone, she was stationed at the copy machine. She was so bored that she started going on to silly websites, like one that calculated the user's date of death. When she clicked the death calculator button after inputting her personal details, she didn't react in shock: all she thought was, 'Oh, I guess I've done this before.'

Yona knew this screen with its quickly decreasing numbers. She had probably visited the website a few years ago on a day similar to today. That was when the monitor's digital clock had begun to count down. The clock, measuring the passing of time to the second, even the fraction of a second, broadcast Yona's slowly extinguishing life. Over the past few years, during which time she had forgotten about the site, the clock hadn't stopped once. Today, once again, Yona had satisfied her sporadic curiosity about life expectancy. She marvelled at the numbers shrinking before her.

Yona sat in front of the timer that would someday reach zero and considered how a single second could decide one's fate. Hadn't Yona heard that whenever a fatal fire broke out at a New Year's Eve party, most bodies were found at the cloakroom? If a fire started, if the earth began to shake, if an alarm sounded, you were supposed to stop everything you were doing and run outside. Small actions like looking for your coat or grabbing your bag, like saving the data on your laptop or pressing buttons on your phone: they divided the living and the dead.

Yona's current situation was a disaster, and she was going to have to treat it like one of the disasters she researched for Jungle. She needed to look back at the actions that had driven her into the situation. Maybe it was a seemingly insubstantial event, but one that she couldn't overlook, that had led her to a yellow card. She couldn't clearly remember the time before Kim's sexual harassment, but she knew the origin of her current malaise was definitely Kim. After leaving work, Yona sent an email to Human Resources. She received a reply shortly after. Choi, from HR, said that she would buy Yona dinner.

Choi was one of the rare older women at Jungle. She didn't seem like an employee, and it was easy to talk to her. When Choi asked Yona what she wanted to eat, Yona felt at ease. Choi paid attention to simple things like choosing the menu for their meal. Yona decided on Pyeongyang-style cold noodles and boiled beef. After asking Yona if she'd like any alcohol, Choi ordered a bottle of soju as well. Yona's lips felt heavy as she began to explain her situation.

'Like I said in my email,' she said, 'it's about programme team three's leader, Jo-gwang Kim.'

'Oh, Jo-schlong!' Choi exclaimed.

Yona was surprised by Choi's response, but her familiarity with the issue allowed the conversation to continue smoothly. Choi said that she knew exactly how Yona felt.

'Kim hasn't just caused problems once or twice,' she explained. 'I've had to deal with him a lot.'

'He must have a lot of enemies, then,' Yona mused.

'Well, he does,' Choi replied, 'but everyone's too embarrassed to call themselves his enemy, so there's no backlash. It's like a battle between an elephant and an ant.'

'Have you heard the rumours?' Yona asked. 'That the people Kim touches are already on their way out?'

That was what Yona was most curious about.

'Well,' said Choi, 'I'm only familiar with the employees who've contacted me for help. But if the victims do end up being fired, I imagine it *would* be because they spoke up. How many people in the company could fight with Kim and stay?'

Two hours later, two more bottles of soju were empty, and Choi could speak frankly.

'Yona, I'm telling you this because you remind me of my younger sister,' she said. 'Put the issue behind you.'

The soju stung Yona's throat as she took another sip, but she knew the stinging wasn't the only thing she had to ignore. Choi said one last thing.

'This kind of incident happens all the time. You can press charges and turn it into a problem, but in the long term, that will just make things hard for you, Yona. Kim's a snake: he's always got away with transgressions. If you can't take the heat, get out of the kitchen.'

Yona had a tendency to bob her head when she was listening to someone speak, and the speaker inevitably interpreted the nod as agreement. That's what happened now. Choi took Yona's gesture to mean that Yona wasn't going to go after Kim, and she gave her an approving pat on the shoulder. By the time they had emptied another bottle of soju together, Yona really did agree with Choi's advice.

Complaints made to HR were guaranteed confidential, but victims who shared a harasser somehow learned about each other's existence. Several days later, Yona began to receive messages from people who said that they were 'in solidarity' with her. She met four of them (three women and one man) after work one evening, at a restaurant quite far from the office. She could only guess how they had found her.

'We have to use this opportunity to oust Kim,' one of the other victims exclaimed. 'We tried to do it two years ago, but we weren't prepared and lost the case. Since then, we've been biding our time. We heard that you've been dealing with the same issues as us, Manager Ko, and of course we feel nothing but empathy for you, but we're also reassured.'

They were asking her to help prosecute Kim, but Yona wasn't convinced by them. As she listened, Yona wondered if rumours about the targets of Kim's sexual harassment really were just rumours. Yona was the most senior person at the dinner. The others seemed to draw comfort from the fact that she was a top programming coordinator, but she felt just as burdened by them as she did by Kim. The group told her their stories, and she realised she was lucky that

Kim had only targeted her three times. Some of the victims had suffered more explicit molestation and serious physical violations. Compared to them, Yona had scarcely been touched.

The most desperate-looking person at the table spoke directly to Yona.

'Next Monday, we're going to hold a protest in the lobby,' he said. 'All the victims will be on strike, so it won't seem like we have anything to hide. We're not the people who need to be ashamed – it's that bastard Jo-gwang Kim, isn't it? Manager Ko, join us, please.'

'I'm sorry, there's been a misunderstanding,' Yona replied nervously. 'Something unsavoury did happen to me, but I don't know if I'd call it sexual harassment. I think I misunderstood Mr Kim's intentions.'

Everyone looked surprised by Yona's statement. The desperate man spoke again.

'Team leader, we all saw it.'

This time, it was Yona who was surprised.

'There are multiple CCTVs in the office,' he said. 'You may not realise it, but for all you know, everyone in the building knows what happened to you. If you try to hide something like this, something that every-one's talking about, our situation only becomes more awkward.'

Yona grew uncomfortable hearing the man say 'our situation'. She tried to think of a prior engagement as an excuse to escape.

'We know you're embarrassed,' he continued. 'But that's even more of a reason for us to pool our strength. We'll get in touch. You need time to think.'

Yona hurriedly replied, 'All right,' and stood up from her chair. She pushed open the door to their private dining room and walked out into the hallway, but she couldn't find her shoes. The restaurant consisted of private booths lined up against a central corridor, and customers had to remove their footwear before entering the rooms. It seemed that another customer had left wearing Yona's shoes.

'This is why you should have put your shoes on the rack,' the owner of the restaurant grumbled to Yona. 'Our customers are always losing their possessions, especially recently. What will you do without your shoes?'

The owner made more of a fuss than necessary looking for the missing sneakers and opened the door to the room full of Kim's victims. One of the people inside offered to go out and buy Yona a pair of shoes to wear to her next destination, but Yona just wanted to get as far away as possible from everyone in there. She forcefully declined and decided to borrow a pair of rough slippers from the restaurant for the time being.

The shoes she had lost were actually part of a pair and a half. The store she'd bought them from offered a second right shoe for free with the purchase of each pair. If only the first two of her three shoes hadn't been stolen at the restaurant, the remaining survivor wouldn't have taunted her from the hallway of her apartment when she got home. But the leftover single shoe reminded her of the group of victims and of Kim, and it made her anxious.

Yona received several emails and phone calls after the meal, but she didn't answer them. She would rather not accept the fact that she'd been sexually harassed. Neither did she want to stand unashamed in the lobby and attack Kim. More specifically, she had no desire to join the group of victims, the has-beens and the losers, the dregs of the company. She thought again of what they had told her about the CCTV, that everyone already knew what had happened to her.

On the day of the protest, Yona ran into them in the lobby, holding a large banner. They didn't cover their faces, but Yona unwittingly hid hers as she passed by them. The protesters were disciplined within a few days. That night, Yona threw out her third shoe.

'Please, just take it,' Yona's co-worker said, handing her the customer service call. The man on the phone kept asking, 'Why can't I?' over and over again. *Why can't I cancel the trip?* was what he meant. 'Why can't you hang up?' Yona wanted to say in response. As she listened to the man speak, she forgot her prepared script for dealing with customers. The person with whom this man was planning to travel had died.

'Is it a direct relative?' Yona asked. 'The person you were going to travel with.'

'No, she's not,' he answered.

'Let me check our policy and I'll call you back.'

Yona unnecessarily asked for the man's phone number a second time and hung up. She didn't want to, but she *had* told him that she would check on his case.

The cancellation of this trip depended entirely upon Yona. If she decided to, she could cancel without a fee, although of course Jungle officially discouraged doing such a thing. But how could someone go on holiday after his travel partner had died? Yona decided that she would cancel the trip for the man. But that afternoon, a brochure for the Jinhae trip landed on Yona's desk. Its acknowledgements page bore the name of a co-worker from another team. Yona was filled with such feverish anger that she couldn't sit inside the office any longer. She left work early, before she could file a cancellation request.

Yona usually took three different subway lines on her way home, even though she could get home by taking only two. Over the past few years, the possible routes between Jungle's office and her apartment had increased. Stations dotted the city with greater density, new lines had emerged and existing lines had expanded to neighbouring towns. It varied a bit depending on which route she took, but travel time between Yona's apartment and work kept decreasing. This surprised Yona, because now there were more stations than ever. In spite of her shortened commute, the typical journey home felt lengthier and even more boring than before. It was exhausting, too, that in spite of so many new lines, train cars were always packed during rush hour. The city was satiating its ravenous hunger by pulling more and more people into its belly. Yona's phone rang. It was the customer who had called her that morning, already forgotten in the midst of Yona's distress. *Didn't he say that his travel companion had died?* She had told him she would cancel his trip, because of course he couldn't go now. She was angry with the man for following her home by phone, but more than that, she resented Jungle for giving out her mobile phone number so people could call her after hours. Yona gave the man the following verdict:

'Refunds are only possible in the case of death of the purchaser,' Yona said as she was swept up into a large crowd. 'This means that the person you planned to travel with can cancel for a refund, but if *you* cancel, you won't get your money back.' The man hung up. Yona looked at the subway map. Lines under construction suffocated the city with one new stop after another. Yona wanted to set the end of one of the subway lines on fire, like using a match to stop a run in a sweater. She wanted the threads to stop unravelling.

Summer began. It had been a while since flowers fell off the trees, and in their place black cherries were now plummeting to the ground, so that the pavements were covered with juicy bruises. Yona finally sent in her resignation letter.

'Be honest,' Kim said as he grabbed a drink for her from the coffee machine. 'Do you need a break, or are you looking for another job?'

It was a fitting question.

'I just need to rest for a bit,' Yona said. 'I haven't been feeling well recently.'

Kim nodded. Who knew if Yona was repeating the words of so many employees before her?

'Even so, I can't really let you go, can I?' Kim asked.

Yona quietly looked at the ground.

'Why don't we do this – I'll give you a month's break, and for the first couple of weeks you'll go on a trip,' Kim announced. 'Not as an employee, but as a customer. Several of our packages are currently in the middle of review, and we're trying to decide if we'll continue to offer them or if they should be discontinued. You pick one of these, and we'll cover the entire trip like it's a business expense. After you come back, all you have to do is write a one-page report about your travels. You've been working here for ten years – you must be tired.'

'Can my position be vacant for a month?' Yona enquired.

'It'll be a break for you, but Jungle sees it as a business trip, so don't worry. I'll use your report to decide whether or not to terminate the package.'

'Are any of the trips I designed at risk of termination?'

'Um, no.' Kim looked irritated.

'So I'm making a final decision about someone else's project?'

'Can anyone objectively judge a trip that he or she designed? We have to perform evaluations like this sometimes. I'm in charge of the trips in question. Aren't you a top programming coordinator, someone I can trust? Your time away might be a holiday, but it's still part of your work duties. Understand?'

Yona looked at Kim with wide-eyed surprise, and he softened his tone.

'When I'd been at Jungle for about ten years, my

boss did this for me, too. I accepted the offer for a free trip, of course, but I'd realised by then what a cold-blooded company this place is. Thankfully, the timing works out well with your attempted resignation. Just think of this as a thank-you gift for your years of service.'

Yona hadn't submitted her resignation letter with the absolute intention of quitting. It just seemed like if she didn't send Kim some sort of signal, he would bully her even more. At Jungle, a holiday didn't mean a brief, comma-like pause. It was an action that indicated finality: the full stop at the end of a sentence. Only when someone was on the brink of exhaustion did the company start to throw days off at him or her in all sorts of circuitous ways. Otherwise, you never knew when you'd get time off. Occasionally, though, the full stop *was* a comma: a break between intervals of feverish devotion to one's work. If you were a necessary employee, someone Jungle wanted to hold on to, they didn't just let you wallow dissatisfied until you resigned. Before granting her a break, Jungle needed to find out whether Yona really was considering leaving. Finally, she thought, they'd reached a silent agreement. Kim was trading in his wrongdoings for the offer of a no-strings-attached business trip. If only he hadn't brushed Yona's waist twice as the conversation ended, she almost could have forgotten his earlier remarks about his Johnson.

Yona glanced over descriptions of Jungle's current destinations. *Experience the Ashen Red Energy of a Volcano! Feel Mother Earth Tremble. Ride Noah's Ark and*

Be the Judge of the Seas. Tsunamis: Calamity and Horror Before Your Eyes. Not one of the ten most popular trips was attributed to Yona, even though the Jinhae expedition was obviously hers. After planting and nurturing the seeds for the trip, undergoing all sorts of hardship as she fertilised its field, she didn't even get to experience the fruits of her labour. Right before she could harvest the crop, the trip had been handed over to another employee. Just looking at the description of Jinhae and its cherry blossoms made Yona's blood sizzle with anger. That trip now ranked seventh in sales. Yona's replacement had essentially been given an already-complete project. He was probably dilly-dallying about right now, oh-so pleased with himself. She got even angrier.

Yona had five trips to choose from. Fortunately, none of her own projects were at risk of removal, even if she wasn't getting credit. Yona's trips usually lay somewhere in between the most and least popular destinations. She tried to learn more about her holiday options by speaking with an adviser in the customer service centre. As soon as Yona said that she was trying to decide among five trips, the adviser unsurprisingly suggested the most expensive one.

'I'm going to recommend Desert Sinkhole,' the adviser said confidently. 'The accommodation is why it's more costly than the other trips. You'll be staying in a newly constructed resort – it's very clean. The trip doubles as an opportunity to relax. It's rare, too, that you can see volcanoes, deserts and hot springs all in the same location. Desert Sinkhole may be twenty per cent more expensive than the other trips, but you'll be twenty per cent more satisfied.'

The adviser's poise betrayed her ignorance. Clearly, she didn't know that a twenty per cent decrease in revenue had put the package she was advertising at the crossroads of life and death. But since Jungle was paying, it seemed appropriate to pick the most expensive option.

The desert sinkhole trip was a six-day package, its destination a place called Mui. Yona had to search on the internet to find where it was. Mui was an island nation about the same size as Korea's Jeju Island. You had to cross the southern part of Vietnam to get there. First you flew to Ho Chi Minh City airport, then you rode a bus to the seaside city of Phan Thiet and finally you took a thirty-minute boat ride. Yona understood why this package wasn't more popular. It took a day to get there and a day to get back, and the scenery upon arrival was significantly less exciting than that of other disaster packages. There was a desert sinkhole like the name suggested, and maybe it was as 'frightening and grim' as the promotional materials claimed, but the problem was that rain had turned the sinkhole into a lake. It didn't really look scary any more, or like anything special at all. When people heard the word 'sinkhole', they at least expected something like the 2010 Guatemala City hole, a five-hundred-metre-deep tumorous pit that had demolished the city's entire downtown. Yona was growing suspicious that Mui wouldn't fulfil her already low expectations. She looked up the flights she would take if she went on the trip.

Desire and interest go hand in hand. When your eyes first scan over a place name on a map, that desire is as small as a bean. But as your interest in a place grows, the bean sprouts into something much more substantial. For the first time in a very long while, Yona remembered that she'd started working at a travel company because she enjoyed travel. Yona had gone on a few international business trips with Jungle, but she primarily worked domestically. She could have taken personal trips during her days off, but whenever she had the time, she no longer wanted to go anywhere. As she thought about the prospect of leaving for another country, even for work, it was like pushing open a window that had been closed for a long time. An unfamiliar, chilly breeze blew through.

Yona pulled out her long-untouched passport. There were actually four passports in her drawer, three expired and one valid. In the first and oldest passport, Yona's photo was as earless as a Paul Klee self-portrait. The photos in her newer passports progressively showed more and more of Yona's ears and eyebrows. She didn't know if it was evolution or regression, but regardless, they showed more of Yona's face. Yona hadn't even decided the dates for her trip yet, but she pulled out a suitcase and pre-emptively put her passport and camera inside.

If disaster were to break apart the Earth during Yona's trip, her camera was the tool that would make the shattered pieces around her feel real. The moment the camera shutter clicked, the image in front of it was no longer a subject or landscape to photograph.

It was a blank space in time. Sometimes short inter-vals of nothingness affected people more than long periods of actual life. Yona considered how trips began. Didn't travellers begin their journeys before they'd even left? Travel was nothing more than the recognition of the path they were already on.

Time passed slowly, and Yona dealt with things she had to do before her trip started. One of her tasks was the cancellation for the man she'd spoken with twice. She'd changed her mind again and wasn't going to charge him for it. In order to withdraw his trip, she had to send in five whole pages of documents. She could only cancel in the first place thanks to a loop-hole in Jungle's system, and the stress of the ordeal was burning a hole in Yona's throat.

Departure was at the beginning of July. Even though more than a week remained before she left, Yona began to place things in her bag with a sudden urgency, as if she'd forgotten about them until now. She packed mosquito repellent, emergency medicine, and pencils and candy to give to local children. Con-stipation and diarrhoea pills were necessities, too. As she packed, it felt like so many things were vital. Barely a day would pass after she had closed the bag before she found a new reason to open it, as she thought of something else to pack. Soon after, she would open her suitcase yet again to remove other items, like her toothbrush, that she still needed before leaving for her trip. Yona spent several days stuck between two worlds before closing the suitcase for good the morning of departure.

Now Yona was inside the aeroplane as she had long envisioned. She pulled a blanket up to her neck and looked through the cornerless window. Lights below her dotted the Earth like a mosaic. Looking from above, she could see that the city was at full capacity. Only inside this obese metropolis could one take the congestion for granted. As the red-eye flight cruised overhead, the urban swarm shrank into nothingness.

2

The Desert Sinkhole

–

SIX TRAVELLERS SPENT THREE HOURS rushing over Vietnam's national highway number one. The bus they were riding had been swept up in a deluge of motorcycles. Motorcycles zipped along the road, and more waited by the kerb. The kerbside bikers were waiting for scheduled pickups, or hanging around hoping for customers. Bikes carrying up to four people at a time could be seen from the bus windows. Yona also watched the passing Vietnamese flags, stuck in the ground at equal distances, and street vendors hawking bags of bread and noodles. Two-storey houses, simple except for their beautifully decorated eaves and elaborate front gates, glided by, alongside tangles of electrical lines that resembled thick hair. The travellers recorded each moment, clicking their camera shutters as they glanced out of the windows at an outdoor wedding, and later when they drove past a cemetery busy with funeral-goers.

Among all the views on the road, what caught Yona's eye most was the Korean writing. She saw Korean words written on small items, like vests labelled with the phrase 'quick delivery' and T-shirts with unexpected slogans like 'hazardous materials vehicle', but she also noted Korean on buses, like those adorned with misspellings such as 'automatic rood' instead of 'automatic door'.

'Right now in Vietnam, we have a lot of buses covered with maps of the old Seoul transportation system,' the guide explained. 'People import old Korean buses to Vietnam, and buses with even a few Korean words on them sell for more. This means that a lot of people just go ahead and put Korean stickers on the vehicles they're selling. If you look carefully, you'll see Korean letters all over the place, even though what's written doesn't always make sense. Recently I rode a bus that, according to the map on the outside of the vehicle, went by Jungang Market, Gyeongbokgung Palace and Mapo-gucheong. Of course, that wasn't the actual route. Isn't that funny?'

The guide had energy suitable for a person used to long journeys. Her name, she said, was 'Lou', and she was Korean – even if her name wasn't. She spent ten months each year in places like Vietnam, Mui and Cambodia, but Mui was her favourite. Accommodation there was of especially high quality, she said.

Highway one first hit the coast at the seaside town of Phan Thiet. The town was a checkpoint you had to pass through to reach Mui. The bus stopped in front of the entrance to Phan Thiet's largest grocery store. Lou rose from the passenger seat.

'We're going to take a break here for the next hour,' she told the travellers. 'There are no large supermarkets in Mui, so buy any necessary items or snacks you'll want to bring with you.'

An hour later, the passengers boarded carrying remarkably similar purchases: products like G7 coffee, Oral B toothbrushes and *nep moi*, a Vietnamese rice liquor. Everyone carried bundles of toothbrushes as well. Lou had informed the group that toothbrushes were especially cheap in Vietnam, so they'd all been sure to buy a few, even though some of the travellers had initially laughed at the idea. 'We're on a disaster trip,' they'd exclaimed. 'Aren't toothbrushes a bit too ordinary to bring on an adventure like this?'

'Maybe Mui is more ordinary than we're expecting,' the man facing Yona said. There were two men on the trip. One was a college student who'd just been released from his compulsory military service; he'd been preparing for the trip since the beginning of his conscription. The other man looked to be around forty, but he turned out to be much younger. He was only one year older than Yona, and he told her he was a screenwriter. This was the man sitting across from Yona.

None of his works had been turned into movies yet, but he had sold more than ten screenplays to production companies, and he supported himself with a variety of side jobs. The other two female travellers, besides Lou, were a mother and child. The woman was an elementary school teacher who'd brought along her five-year-old daughter. Yona's fellow adventurers began to ask her questions.

'Are you married yet?' one person asked.

'How old are you?' demanded another.

'What kind of work do you do?'

She couldn't say that she was on a business trip, or that the person who'd created this package was a co-worker. She wondered if their guide, sitting in front of them, was aware of the personal details of her clients. Thankfully, all Lou seemed to know was the contents of everyone's passports. Yona tried to come up with an appropriate fake job for herself. She decided she'd be a thirty-three-year-old independent café owner: a life Yona had daydreamed about. If she ever quit her job at Jungle, Yona really did want to open a store that sold coffee and pie.

'The truth is, I paid for this trip with my student loans,' the college student told the others. 'Trips like this aren't usually expensive, so I figured it wouldn't be too hard on my finances. And the insurance that comes with the package is pretty generous, too: if anything happens to me on this trip, the massive payout Jungle will send my parents is going to pay back the debt I owe them for raising me!'

It seemed like the college student had said this as a joke, but the guide wore a serious look on her face. 'As long as you pay attention to your surroundings, you'll be fine. Accidents that occur because of broken rules aren't covered.'

'Oh, I know, I know,' the boy replied. 'Honestly, I've

always had a lot of interest in trips like this, trips that do good for the local community. My friends all want to go see museums or castles, but I don't care about those things. By the time our trip ends, I want to be inspired to live *dynamically*. Of course, if I die, I'll be helping out my parents financially, at least.'

As soon as the student repeated his joke, Lou clarified once more.

'There's no chance you'll die,' she asserted. 'Our Jungle system isn't something haphazardly cobbled together.'

The college student shook his head in annoyance and turned his gaze to the view outside the window. Yona had discovered two potential problems during the conversation. One was that the trip probably wasn't going to live up to the student's expectation of ethical and locally engaged travel. The other was that Jungle's system didn't actually guarantee safety one hundred per cent. Yona thought of several safety incidents Jungle had dealt with. The causes of death were drowning, car accident and feverish illness; floods, crashes and fevers were not, of course, the disasters the travellers had chosen when planning their trips. The deaths were unadvertised disasters, unexpected by the travellers. From what Yona knew, Lou may have thought her assurances reflected the truth, but that didn't mean there were no accidents. It was just that news didn't spread, or it did so slowly.

They'd begun to pick up the fishy smell of anchovies in Phan Thiet harbour, and it had continued to waft into their nostrils throughout the crossing to

Mui island. Yona breathed in deeply. This smell was probably *nuoc mam*. It was an odour she knew only by sight, a word she'd read in guidebooks. *Nuoc mam*, a kind of fermented anchovies, changed the flavour of any other ingredient it touched. In this part of the world, it was the conqueror of mealtimes. Mui lived by its *nuoc mam*. 'Mui's mornings are filled with the hubbub of fishing, and its nights with the smell of fresh catches fermenting in salt.' That was the first sentence of a book she had read about Mui. But the statement could no longer be written in the present tense, as most of Mui's labour force had left for nearby Vietnam and *nuoc mam* was now made in Phan Thiet. Even so, you could certainly still smell in it Mui.

Yona didn't mind the fishiness. Like the stimulating odour that hit your nose when entering a musty house, or a new place, it lasted only a moment. Most people grew used to the smell of their new surroundings, and never again experienced the exciting initial pungency.

The bus drove down a road lined with gingko trees. Mui was already dark. It wasn't easy to see what lay at the end of the road. Once Mui had drifted into night, you couldn't see a single thing on the island, not even neon signs from a red light district. The total blackness made the entrance to their lodgings seem even brighter. The bus stopped in front of a resort called 'Belle Époque', whose sign stated that it was a 'Gift From Nature: Private Beach Resort; All Rooms With Ocean Views'.

'It's nice to meet you all. Welcome to Mui.'

The manager, a local, greeted them in fluent Korean. Yona crossed the lobby and looked at the far-off ocean. The resort's rooms consisted of individual bungalows that stood above the ocean on stilts; a twenty-metre wooden bridge connected the cabins to the beach-front. Yona's bungalow was right on the beach. An employee opened the door to her room and began to show Yona around. Her accommodation featured curtains that opened and closed automatically, a TV and speakers, a minibar, a safe and customisable lighting: nothing out of the ordinary for a luxury resort. Next, the employee pressed a button on the remote control in his hand as he introduced one of the resort's 'unique features'. The button turned on two enormous lights, shaped like a pair of eyes, which hung next to the front door on the outside of the cabin.

'You can use these eyes to express your wishes,' the employee explained. 'If you close both, it means "do not disturb", and if you open them, it means "please clean".'

The night was deep, and inside their bungalows, the travellers adjusted to unfamiliar darkness. Most of the rooms were set to 'do not disturb', but the eyes on the teacher's bungalow opened and closed repeatedly. Yona could see the woman's daughter leaning against their window as she pressed buttons on the remote over and over again.

Yona sunk into her sofa. The white linens on her bed looked clean enough to wrap her body in them without worry. On one side of the tub, there was a bag filled with rose petals, and the ocean dozed a few metres below. Yona hadn't had a break like this in a long time. This might be a better trip than I expected, she thought. It was an unfamiliar feeling, thinking that she could miss this place after she left. She mused about the expectations that travellers carried: the expectation of the unexpected, and of freedom from the weight of the everyday. She considered the possibilities that travel presented as the night went on.

The morning sea was black, and silence permeated the air. Nothing dampened Yona's cheerful mood as she went to breakfast. Waves lapped against each other melodiously, and the sunshine beat down gently. It was early, but several people who looked to be locals were tidying the garden. They said hello to Yona.

Yona seemed to be the first guest in the dining hall. The host directed her to the seat with the best view of the ocean. She was offered coffee and black tea, and chose coffee. She decided to eat a fried egg instead of an omelette or scrambled eggs. The cook asked her if she'd like both sides of her egg fried or just one, and she chose the latter.

The writer suddenly approached Yona's table and sat down across from her. 'They're asking us how well they should fry our eggs! Such a light-hearted thing to worry about, isn't it? If I have to choose between an egg fried on one side and an egg fried on both sides, I'll eat anything they give me. Normally, I'm happy as long as I don't burn the egg. Right?'

His coffee and omelette soon arrived. After taking a sip of coffee, he continued.

'I've heard that there are two hundred people working here.'

'Really?' Yona replied. 'I didn't realise it was so many. Are they all hiding?'

The writer didn't answer her question. 'None of the people *I've* seen really seem to be trying very hard at their jobs. It's like they're weirdly optimistic about whatever menial labour they're doing. Our guide told me that the resort's hardest-working employees make ten times more money than everyone else. Of course, she also told me that the best employees work ten times more than the others.'

'Huh,' said Yona. 'I guess the manager we met yesterday is a high earner, then.'

'Lou told me that the manager earns more than three million won per month. If you think about the cost of living here, it's a really powerful salary. But it looks like the resort hasn't had many customers recently. We're the only guests right now. I don't mind, cause it makes it feel like we've rented out the entire place, but the overstock of food inventory must be a headache for them.'

He ate his omelette, shaped like a half moon, in three bites. The garden visible outside was still in the midst of landscaping.

'You should eat a lot,' the writer urged Yona. 'Our schedule today is really full.'

'Have you ever been to a desert like the one we're going to?' Yona asked him.

'I have – a few times, actually. Take care getting dressed before we go out. When you're in the desert, the sand is so fine that it sticks to bare skin and makes you feel like you're a steak marinating in salt and pepper. That's what you'll feel like if you don't cover yourself.'

The writer polished off a second plate of omelette as he said this. He seemed to be living life in fast-forward, whether he was eating or walking or talking. The teacher and her daughter arrived as Yona and the writer stood up to leave. Lou and the college student ate last. Yona didn't see any other guests at the resort.

The desert was in the northern part of the island. The group of travellers divided in two, and each group boarded a different SUV. They weren't the only ones traversing the road that circled Mui. Local children ran around in huge groups as they waved their arms, several of them chasing the cars, and a herd of cattle ambled across the road, their large bodies undulating like ridges of sand from the dunes far off in the distance. And then the desert rushed into view.

Sunglasses came in handy with the sandstorms swirling in the air, but Yona wanted to experience the desert's true colours, so she took hers off. The white sands and neighbouring forest, of dark blue palm trees, were as distinctly delineated as the stripes in a two-colour flag. As the azure sea rose into view, the flag became tricoloured. Soon it consisted of countless shades beyond the original three. The desert seemed to be dividing itself into innumerable patches of subtly unique hues. Yona realised for the first time how many colours were needed to describe the appearance of a desert, and how its saturation and brightness varied. As deviations appeared in the sand, the colour of the desert changed, as did the desert's name. There was the white sand desert and the red sand desert. Even if you stood in one spot, the sand's shade varied depending on how many clouds hung overhead, and whether or not sunlight was beating through the clouds. Yona couldn't pull her eyes away from the sight. She wondered how a place ravaged by disaster could look so peaceful.

'Right now, we're at the white sand desert,' the guide explained to the group. 'It's been the home to two Mui tribes, the Kanu people and the Unda people, for centuries, and they've fought frequently throughout history. In 1963, in this very desert, the Kanu used farming tools to massacre the Unda. It was revenge for the Unda taking their land. By the end of the bloodshed, it's said there were about three hundred Unda heads scattered across the desert. Their heads were removed from their dead bodies as part of a practice called head hunting. On the first night of the massacre, an enormous rainstorm hit the area, and four days later, on Sunday morning, another incident occurred. A circle-shaped portion of the white desert collapsed, like an enormous crater had been drilled into the earth.'

'At the time,' the guide continued, 'everyone thought it was a curse from the gods, but nowadays people know that it was a sinkhole, a natural phenomenon that can occur in deserts. Anyhow, the heads littered throughout the area rolled into the sinkhole, which was apparently one hundred and eighty metres deep. In the meantime, the Kanu started a second massacre, killing people throughout the village. Now this area is beautiful, but it's the site of tragedy, too.'

The teacher's daughter listened diligently to the guide's explanation, her eyes sparkling. To think that there had once been a hole filled with heads, right here. But the girl couldn't actually see the hole occupying her imagination. That was because the sinkhole had filled up with water and was now a wide lake. People called this place the head lake, but now instead of heads, lotuses were floating on its surface. Even after she was told that the hole was now a body of water, the child kept asking where the cut-off heads were. The guide showed the group pictures of the 1963 tragedy, but the hazy black-and-white photos didn't hold her interest. Other than the girl, everyone's expressions were serious.

'Isn't this the reason we're on this trip?' the teacher asked. 'To avoid repeating history?' The writer nodded his head.

They sat down at a rest stop with a view of the lake and cooled their sweaty bodies. Wide-eyed children approached and attempted to sell them knick-knacks: bracelets, pipes and dolls. Some of the children carried younger siblings on their backs, and others shielded the travellers from the hot sun with large parasols. A few of the vendors broke into the crowd of foreigners before almost instantly running away in surprise. The owner of the rest stop glared sternly at the children; then, even though they had run into a corner dejectedly, they returned, shouting, 'One dollar! One dollar!'

'What's that?' Yona asked, about a building in the distance.

The guide explained that the building Yona was looking at actually stood in the red sand desert. She said that a tower was under construction there. It was supposed to house an observatory where visitors could look down at both the desert and the sea, but there was no way the tower would be finished. Yona had heard about this project: apparently, construction was suspended and the company erecting the structure had given up. In several ways, Mui was frozen like this.

Yona's first reaction to the desert was a sudden urge to touch. But even if she reached her arms out in the hope of grasping some scenic silhouette, the only thing that would remain in her hand afterwards was a fistful of sand. Yona climbed up on to a slope of the fine material as if trying to quench her thirst for touch. The group had followed an experienced-looking elderly woman who'd joined them at some point, and now they were all standing at the top of the sand hill. The woman stood behind Yona and held a sled out to her. It looked like a repurposed plastic board. The teacher's daughter rode the sled down the dunes several times.

The guide introduced the elderly woman. 'This person is the relative of a head-hunting victim from 1963. She says that she makes a living working with tourists.'

Yona wanted to take a picture of the wrinkled woman, with eyes too deep-set to read. As soon as Yona pointed her camera at her, the woman said, 'One dollar.' All of a sudden, she began to pose zealously like a model, and as a result, the picture didn't come out well. Yona finally managed to snap a picture of the woman walking away after she'd stopped trying to entertain.

The teacher's daughter was squatting on the beach in front of the bungalows. After briefly fiddling with something, she ran back several metres. In the place where the child had been crouched, firecrackers resembling sticks of dynamite exploded with a lightning-like flash and a thunderous clap. Her mother ran up, pulled the girl away, and smacked her on the bottom. When asked where she'd got firecrackers, the girl answered that another child at the rest stop had given them to her.

Yona went to the spot that the child had fled. The tips of the extinguished fireworks were blackened, and ants swarmed nearby. The explosives seemed to have been dropped on an anthill. Other beach-dwelling insects scurried around as well. Yona threw the remains into a bin and then paced around the area for a while, until the girl sprinted back over without her mother. Like a criminal returning to the scene of the crime, she was scanning the ground to find where the firecracker had detonated. But Yona had already removed it, and as the waves neared the resort in footstep-length increments, the hole where the firecracker had been lodged was also filling with water.

'The ants got hurt,' Yona admonished the girl. 'The other bugs, too.'

'Did their heads fall off?'

Yona didn't know how to answer the innocent-looking child. Without waiting for an answer, the girl began to frantically trample the ants over and over again.

'I have to do a second massacre ...' she said.

'You can't – then the bugs will get even more hurt,' Yona warned. 'We all have to live together. Don't we?'

'Huh? The healthy ants are carrying away the hurt ones. Look, right there!'

The girl poked at the bugs with a small tree branch that had been lying on the ground. The sand wasn't firm like asphalt; it yielded under the stick's pressure, to the dismay of the ants trying to hide under the surface. As the child mumbled to herself, 'Unda ants, die,' Yona wondered if Jungle should impose age limits on disaster trips. The girl was still 'massacring' the ants. Yona recalled cutting open the stomachs of crickets and grasshoppers with a box cutter when she was younger.

'But why are there so many bugs?' the girl asked Yona. 'They all came out of the ground.'

As soon as the girl stopped speaking, thick raindrops began to fall from the sky. Yona grabbed the girl's hand and they ran inside the resort.

Guests watched the streaks of rain pour down as they enjoyed afternoon tea. The manager was preparing coffee with condensed milk. Droplets of coffee made a knocking noise as they drip-drip-dripped into a cup full of ice. As Yona quietly watched, it felt like time stopped with each drop of coffee hitting its target.

'I've been taking my daughter everywhere with me since she was one,' the teacher declared at a nearby table. 'People always tell me that kids won't remember travel from when they're babies, but whenever we return from a trip, I can see with my own eyes that she's grown. She tries foods that she wouldn't have eaten before, she's not afraid to use tools and gadgets like an adult, she can independently do things that she used to need help with – seeing all that, I try to visit somewhere new every school holiday, for her as much as for me.'

After saying this, the teacher saw her daughter come in soaking wet and hurried out of her seat. She left the table, explaining that she'd have the child change and then both of them would come back. The writer continued the conversation. He said that he'd originally planned on taking a trip to Centralia, but then he'd changed his mind and come here instead. Centralia was a town in the United States that had been on fire for the past fifty years. Embers had set the town's vein of underground coal ablaze, and the asphalt above it was now completely melted. Most residents had left.

'Isn't the movie *Silent Hill* about that town?' Yona asked. 'I was curious about the place, too, but apparently it'll take two and hundred fifty more years for the coal to completely burn up, so I figured I still have time to go.'

'You know a lot about holiday spots,' the writer replied, impressed. He said that he'd put off the trip for the same reason, and excitedly shared more of his travel knowledge with Yona. The college student occupied himself with the Wi-Fi available only at the resort. He was reading news articles on his phone.

'Apparently a basketball was discovered off the coast of Japan,' he said.

'A basketball?' Yona asked.

'It's wreckage from the Jinhae tsunami. The story says that a basketball, with the name of some kid from Jinhae written on it, was discovered near the shoreline. I guess it was heading towards Japan.'

'Well, you don't need to go somewhere that far away to find relics of disaster,' Yona replied. 'It's not just Japan now; our country's not exactly safe from tsunamis either, any more.'

'All of the southern coast was ruined in the Jinhae tsunami,' someone at the table said.

'Then why did we come all the way here?' the teacher asked. She was already back from sorting out her daughter.

'It's too scary to visit disaster destinations close to home,' Yona explained. 'Don't we need to be distanced somewhat from our ordinary lives – from the blankets we sleep under, and the bowls we eat from every day – in order to see the situation more objectively?'

People seemed to agree with Yona. The discussion went on for a while. Participants unleashed their vast disaster trip expertise – and their appreciation for them, too – until eventually the guide spoke up, reminding them that the very trip they were on was a disaster trip.

'Tomorrow we're going on a volcano tour,' she informed them. 'Be done with breakfast and ready in the lobby by 10 a.m.'

The travellers were in high spirits after returning from the desert, but it seemed like they'd seen Mui's highlights too early. When Yona glanced at the itinerary, everything looked dull. Who had come up with such a poorly organised schedule? Yona understood why this trip was targeted for cancellation.

'Imagine the mixture I mentioned earlier plunging deep into the earth,' the guide said the next day as they made their way to Mui's volcano. She wasn't done talking about the sinkholes, even if they were no longer in the desert. 'It's a particularly unusual geological cocktail that leads to disasters like the holes we saw yesterday. Okay, everyone, we've reached the entrance to the volcano. You remember the safety precautions, right? You can't walk on top of the lava. Even if it looks hard on the outside, the inside is still boiling. An American tourist died here in 1903, and five others were injured. Clouds of volcanic ash can travel down the side of this volcano at speeds of one hundred kilometres per hour. The internal temperature of the clouds reaches several hundred degrees. If you fall into one of them, you'll probably be burned alive. Within five minutes, juices from your flesh will be dripping out of your body. And volcanic rock is sharp as razors, so don't just carelessly sit down on the ground.'

But the guide's words seemed empty. The warning sign posted at the entrance to the volcano tried hard to re-enact the horrors of the past, but the atmosphere didn't live up to such sombre descriptions. On one side of the group, local children were rolling around on the ground playing. Korean-style street stalls by the volcano's entrance stood ready to alleviate hunger. The available snacks included ramen and bowls of rice. Since Yona and the others were the only tourists, they felt a touch of guilt and decided to purchase some of the foods. Children hawked flowers and woodcrafts they'd carved themselves. Sometimes they showed off their business acumen by including a free postcard or two with the wooden carvings. They also sold picture postcards separately, but the scenery depicted in the cards wasn't from here. Yona saw a postcard featuring Indonesia's Mount Merapi, brazenly being sold here in Mui. She was again reminded why Jungle wanted to cancel this trip.

The guide stood tiredly in front of this sparse display of wares, like she had to promote the spread herself. She was describing the volcano's most recent eruption, which had happened years ago. But it seemed like she hadn't witnessed it first hand, based on her lacklustre retelling.

'I wish she'd just be quiet. What she's saying is all talk, and this is, well ...' Yona trailed off.

The writer looked disappointed, too.

'If we hadn't been expressly told, would we even know this was a volcano?' Yona asked. 'It's not obvious at all.'

'And doesn't this geyser just seem like a neighbour-hood well?' the teacher added, describing a source of water bubbling in front of them.

The group stood by the so-called geyser and flipped coins into it. The gurgling fountain taking their money wasn't even hot; its water had long cooled. Local children helped the tourists on their trek to the volcano's peak. The youngsters skilfully set the travellers on horses, some by themselves and others with a partner. They guided Yona and the others to the summit, after slipping a flower into each of their hands. The horse's hooves tick-tocked rhythmically, like a metronome. The college student accidentally dropped his flower. It hit the ground, and a flower-sized cloud of dust spouted into the air. Soon the gift was buried beneath a horse's footprint.

Standing in front of the volcano's crater, the group took pictures, made wishes and threw their flowers like they were bouquets. The bouquets drew an arc as they fell into the crater. To Yona, the whole action felt like neatly placing rubbish into its specific waste receptacle. Watching the flowers fall was less than thrilling. She just wanted white-grey volcanic ash to flutter down the mountain, like a cannon salute from some unknown army.

The teacher had brought two sketchbooks. She'd hoped her daughter's passion for art would help transfer events from the trip on to the books' pages, like ink-covered print blocks pressed on to blank sheets of paper. But her daughter didn't make an effort to draw, and only after her mother smacked her bottom a few times did she open up one of the sketchbooks. Her drawings didn't live up to her mother's expectations. The first of the five or so images she quickly scribbled down was of the Brazilian barbecue she'd eaten at the resort, and the last depicted heads, scattered about a crater. The meat didn't at all fit with the purpose of this trip, and the heads were just unpleasant. The bodiless faces in the girl's drawing were all laughing. And they looked familiar, too. Not to mention that there were precisely six of them.

'It's us, Mum!' the girl explained, unnecessarily.

The teacher looked embarrassed, worried that the drawing would cause the group distress. While she was drawing, her daughter hadn't been asking pointless questions like she usually did, which was nice, but if the pictures were going to turn out like this, it seemed preferable for her to be asking questions. Whether they were riding in the car or walking along a Mui road, the girl's infantile questions were ceaseless. At first, her inquisitiveness lightened the mood, but it was gradually starting to arouse irritation among the travellers. The girl asked about almost everything, like she was always trying to get in the last word, and at some point, not just her mum, but also the guide, started answering half-heartedly.

Nowadays, disaster trips didn't stop at the disaster zone; most of them boasted other features as well. There were packages that combined tourism with volunteering, packages that mixed tourism and survival challenges, and packages that offered both tourism and education, with classes in history or science. The teacher kept complaining that she should have picked one of the educational trips.

'Kids nowadays – they grab a snow crab, pull off the legs, and expect there to be cooked meat inside,' she complained. 'If you cut a fish in half, they think that the inside will already be roasted. Making kids learn from nature is the best way to give them real experiences, but the theme here is too vague to actually learn anything.'

'Mum, what's that over there?'

Her daughter cut into the conversation, unable to wait for her to finish talking.

'Mum, look at that yellow truck – where's it going?'

The child's mother didn't know where it was going. Even if she did, her answer wouldn't have been any different.

'I don't see it,' she said.

'Mum, look there – the truck stopped for a moment and now it's going again. It's really fast.'

'I don't see it.'

'Look there, Mum. Now there's a second car.'

'I don't know what you're talking about.'

The vehicle accelerated hurriedly and disappeared, relieving the teacher of having to deal with the situation. The others had closed their eyes. They were sleeping, or pretending to sleep. The girl kept repeating, 'Why, why, why?'

On a disaster trip, travellers' reactions to their surroundings usually went through the following stages: shock → sympathy and compassion, and maybe discomfort → gratefulness for their own lives → a sense of responsibility and the feeling that they'd learned a lesson, and maybe an inkling of superiority for having survived. The stage someone reached depended on the person, but ultimately, adventures like these reinforced a fear of disasters and confirmed the fact that the tourist was, in fact, alive. *Even though I came close to disaster, I escaped unscathed*: those were the selfish words of solace you told yourself after returning home.

But with this desert sinkhole package, Yona wasn't experiencing any of the typical responses to a disaster trip. All she had to look forward to now was the one-night homestay. It was an experience meant to mimic the two days of the 1963 head-hunting tragedy. Here, travellers had to choose between two options.

'You can do the homestay from the Unda perspective, or you can do it from the Kanu perspective,' the guide told them. 'The locations are a little bit different. You just pick which one you want.'

The teacher and her daughter chose Unda, and the writer and college student chose Kanu – just to get away from the girl. The writer urged Yona to come with them, but his pleas made Yona pick the Unda group. They divided up and got into two cars that would take them to their respective homestays. The Unda home was on the course of a river that flowed right by the white sand desert.

When the Unda group arrived at their destination, the guide presented their temporary home. 'This is an Unda residence – from the tribe whose heads were discovered in the sinkhole we saw yesterday.

The house is propped up on stilts over the water. It was built to earn tourism revenue that helps provide education and healthcare for Unda children. Don't venture away from the building, to ensure that we don't have any problems and that no one from the village gets hurt. Our little princess shouldn't go too far from Mum, either, got it?'

The girl pouted her lips and hid behind her mother. She then shouted something utterly nonsensical.

'Mum, the guide said she was going to cut off my head!'

They'd been excited about spending the night in a local house, but the accommodation wasn't much. No longer did the travellers have access to Belle Époque's air conditioning, nor its ample bedding. The biggest shock was the bathroom, which was a lot closer to nature than they would have preferred. But considering that it was constructed especially for tourists, they couldn't complain.

An Unda woman introduced the three to their new surroundings. 'The TV runs on a battery. It doesn't use electricity. Oh, and see that house sitting on a boat over there? During the rainy season, people put their houses on boats like that and move. Rainy season just started.'

Out the window, a beauty salon floated by, as did a boatful of kids in the middle of the school day. Another child, a boy criss-crossing the water in a black plastic washbasin, made eye contact with Yona's party and instantly formed a 'V' sign with his fingers.

'Pretty!' the boy shouted, in Korean, to Yona.

Several children approached the women and brushed the dust off a chair in front of them. It looked like the children cleaned the chairs around here so regularly that there was no time for dust to actually collect.

'How many languages do you think the local kids know?' Yona asked.

The teacher looked at the children compassionately and answered.

'They probably just know the most beautiful words in a lot of languages. The words tourists want to hear – wouldn't that make sense? "Pretty", "cute", "handsome": compliments like those.'

One of the kids saw that there was a Korean girl his age and came up to her, whispering, once again in Korean, that she was pretty. He said this while pointing to her eyebrows, and then the teacher's daughter looked a little bit fearful.

Cheerful children draw attention regardless of where they are, but the child receiving the most interest here wasn't acting cheerful. His eyes were as wet as a lake. When he glanced at Yona and then the teacher with waterlogged eyes, he asked each woman, 'Mum?' The Unda woman hugged the child, looking disillusioned as she explained.

'His mother died recently. The boy hasn't realised it yet.'

The Unda woman explained that the boy's grandmother had just barely survived the sinkhole incident while pregnant, but ultimately, her daughter – his mother – had died of a genetic disorder. Yona and her fellow travellers absorbed the heavy fact that the source of all tragedy was that hole in the ground. The teacher held out her hand to the boy, which prompted him to ask again, 'Mum?' before weakly hugging her. Her daughter approached a dog lying on the ground a little way away, like she found this entire situation too strange to deal with.

It was an old dog that spent most of the time lying prone with its belly in the dirt. The blue hammock that hung behind the animal kept looking like it might brush against the dog's back, but even when the teacher's daughter climbed on to the hammock and rocked in it several times, the dog didn't move a bit. Of course, it wasn't old enough to have experienced the events of 1963, but the dog appeared frozen in time. Even if you pointed a camera at it, its expression didn't change at all.

The Unda woman who'd been acting as their guide introduced herself as Nam. Nam led them around for half the day, explaining how to prepare and eat an Unda meal, from catching a fish to cooking it. When evening came, she brought nail art tools to the lodgings and sat down in front of Yona. Nam's English wasn't bad.

'Unda woman have been skilled with our hands since long ago,' Nam explained. 'We're good at this kind of thing.'

The woman was memorable for her expressions. One person used to scrutinising the hands and feet of strangers, and another who felt awkward entrusting her hands and feet to someone unfamiliar, sat face to face. The task proceeded, and Yona's fingernails and toenails were coloured pink, one by one. Outside, the darkening sun seemed to be spinning round and round, and inside, the wind from the fan rotated around the room at a similar speed.

Night came. Yona carried her camera around and captured images of the inside of the house. Damp bedding, a naked light bulb that drooped like the tongue of someone who'd hanged herself, the rusted roof and a door that looked like it had decided the day it was installed that it wouldn't fit into its frame. Yona couldn't lie down to sleep, maybe because the bedding was wet, so she kept sitting for a while. The biggest drag was, of course, the toilet. Yona didn't believe that she would be able to pull her pants down and expose her buttocks in those dark and clammy unkempt facilities, not even to relieve the past four days of constipation.

Misfortune befell the teacher, too, although not due to the toilet. Her daughter had left a toy at the resort, and it was an error on the teacher's part to think that she'd be okay for one night and two days without it. The girl's toy was nowhere to be seen, and the teacher was stretched thin. The child needed something age-appropriate to play with. The guide held out a pen emblazoned with the image of Pororo the Little Penguin, but to a five-year-old, Pororo was already passé. Maybe she would have accepted it if it had been Tayo the Little Bus or Robocar Poli. But since neither Tayo nor Robocar made an appearance, the child began to grow more and more distracted, and when they went back to their individual rooms after dinner, her lack of focus became even more extreme. She kept looking for a remote control in this house on stilts, to lower the eyelids that she was *sure* were affixed somewhere outside. Dog-tired from trying to calm her ever-moving child, the teacher slept like a rock. She let out a few loud shrieks in her sleep that may have been caused by nightmares or may have been the sounds of slumber. No one approached the house to see what caused the noises.

The next day, the Unda group had to pack their bags right after dawn. The house on stilts that had harboured them for the night looked like a wreck. A re-enactment was under way: everything had been made to resemble the famed night in 1963. A fake head that supposedly belonged to the leader of the massacred Unda tribe now hung in front of their window. Farming tools covered with blood were scattered across the desert sand, and cut-off heads rolled about. Unda women in dishevelled dress approached the travellers and warned them to avoid the heads. Yona began to walk, careful not to step on the heads scattered here and there like jagged stones. The teacher and her daughter started the trek along with Yona. There were several others behind them, mostly people carrying the Jungle party's luggage. The porters didn't even look ten years old. As the sun rose higher and higher in the sky, the desert heated up. Yona had worn sandals with thick heels, but the bottoms of her feet felt as hot as if she were standing on a grill.

They stood at the highest point of the white sand desert and watched a performance unfold below. The Unda were being stabbed, pushed, and tripped by the weapon-wielding Kanu. Of course, it wasn't just the Kanus overpowering the Undas. At one moment, everyone fell into a sand crater made especially for the re-enactment. The crater looked frightful thanks to the sound effects and props and lights, but it didn't seem that dangerous, even as people slid down into it and the play came to its chaotic end. On the other side of the impromptu stage sat the writer and the college student, with a Kanu woman.

When the Jungle travellers reconvened, they realised that their accommodation and meals and activities had been almost identical, regardless of whether they'd chosen Unda or Kanu. They'd met several locals inside a house on stilts, eaten some simple snacks, and then, after watching a traditional performance, they'd slept in similar rooms. The massages and nail art and fishing were the same, too. One other thing was similar: everyone seemed to have been bitten over half their bodies by mosquitoes.

They all wanted to return quickly to the resort, but Yona was the reason they were delayed. One side of the window in the room Yona had stayed in was broken, and it was unclear if had been shattered before they arrived or if it got that way during the night – or if it had been tampered with during breakfast. Thanks to the broken window, the room was now filled with exotic winged insects, and Yona's camera was gone. The writer scrutinised the glass and said that it seemed like someone who knew what they were doing had cut it with a knife. The guide looked uncomfortable, but she dealt with the situation like an expert. First they rummaged through the other houses on stilts, one by one. They looked, of course, at the room where they'd stayed, and then they searched the houses lined up next to it. They discovered three cameras.

'Miss Yona's camera must be one of these,' the guide said.

Before she could even take a look at them, a fourth camera appeared. The fourth was Yona's. The teacher's daughter brought it over.

'This morning, she said I could carry it around with me ...' the child said, as if she was tattling on Yona.

Yona's face turned red, and then she remembered she had done exactly that. As soon as Yona's camera was discovered, the Unda child who'd been in possession of one of the three others burst into tears. It was the same kid who'd made a 'V' sign with his hands while floating by on a plastic washbasin. Yona lowered her burning face.

'I'm sorry,' she told the child. 'I'm embarrassed to have made such a disturbance because of my carelessness.'

Because she was speaking Korean, the crying child couldn't understand, but the important thing for Yona was that her fellow travellers heard. Yona took a small bag of candy out of her bag and held it out to the tearful boy. Then she got in the car like she was running away. The teacher broke the silence flowing throughout the inside of the vehicle. She seemed to be mumbling to herself: 'How could so many kids have cameras in a place like that?' This statement upset the college student. He'd looked uncomfortable ever since the camera hunt began.

'Did we really have to search the homes like that? It was so awkward,' he exclaimed, clearly angry. 'This goes against the whole point of the trip. I'm just saying, we have to keep track of our own things.'

Yona closed her eyes and sat in silence. She did feel apologetic. If she'd lost something smaller than a camera, she wouldn't have bothered to say anything. The college student began to argue with the guide, and Yona watched. The student gave a monologue about the aim of an ethical trip, and finally the guide rebutted that this trip didn't fall under the category of 'ethical tourism'. To stop the two, Yona said, 'It's all my fault. I'm sorry.' The fight quieted, but curses kept coming off the college student's tongue. He was still upset by what the guide had said.

'Mum, what does "fuck" mean?' the teacher's daughter asked, briefly taking a break from drawing.

'You don't need to know,' the teacher replied.

'Mum, Mum, what does "fuck" mean? What does it mean?'

'You know, don't you? Are you really asking because you've never heard that word?'

As she got to the end of the question, the teacher's voice grew quieter, but the child seemed to enjoy listening to her mother's timid explanations, so she answered even more sonorously to taunt her.

'Yeah, I do know what it is!' she shouted. 'It's a bad word, a bad word.'

The writer tried to change the subject by bringing up the Unda skull-shaped decorations he'd bought from a vendor, but no one was interested. The guide just stared at the itinerary. Everyone kept their mouths shut.

'Mum, I want to eat a rice omelette!' the teacher's daughter yelled tactlessly, instantly wrapping up the 'fuck' situation.

The car stopped in front of a restaurant, and soon a lunch that specifically included a rice omelette had been prepared. The college student pounded his chest like he had indigestion. A rash that hadn't been there a few hours ago welled up on Yona's forearm. The unfamiliar water here probably wasn't the only reason for the rash's appearance.

The resort was the sole place in Mui that didn't have a shortage of drinking water. Judging by their experience last night, the travellers had realised that a guest in the resort used more water per day than all the houses on stilts together. After the group ate lunch, they plunged into four hours of volunteer work, drilling a well. The team on the trip right before them had done some work on the well already, and progress continued with the new visitors as if they were competitors in a relay race. The now-silent party dug into the earth as diligently as they could. After four hours, they enjoyed a moment of contentment when, like compensation for their labour, water leaked out of the ground. It wasn't just a reward for the work they'd undertaken; it also seemed like compensation for the emotional toil that had been plaguing everyone since the morning.

Before returning to the resort, they bathed in nearby hot springs to dissolve their fatigue. It was hard to judge the water quality, but because the springs were near a volcano, someone kept loudly claiming, the water had special properties. After two hours, they emerged with skin that was definitely a bit softer, and commemorative stamps on their foreheads: mosquito bites.

After a brief burst of rain, the earth quickly dried out again. Under a sign that said 'Mui Market', the travellers encountered a line of tents and street stalls. They purchased their desired souvenirs, then entered a nearby pub and sat down. The walls were shabby, but it was crowded with locals and had a pleasant atmosphere. There were no menus, so you couldn't know exactly what they sold. The guide ordered food and drink for the group. At the end of the alley outside the bar, locals knelt as they braided clients' hair, and others gave people tattoos. A huge bundle of balloons came into view. The bundle looked like a bouquet of flowers, ready to shoot up into the night sky. The guide bought two balloons and gave one to Yona and the other to the teacher's daughter. The writer came back to the group holding a dragon fruit, which he began to cut in two. After spooning out the flesh and eating it, he filled the remaining pink skin with *nep moi*, a local spirit.

'These are dragon fruit shots,' he said, pouring the alcoholic creation into cups for the others. 'Let's drink it all in one go! Days like today make us all feel on edge, don't they? Let's drink and unwind a little.'

The teacher's daughter touched her tongue to the dragon fruit alcohol and then pretended to be drunk, which took some members of the group aback and made others smile. Soon, even the college student's expression had softened. They didn't want to accept that they'd gone on a trip to a disaster zone only to create a disaster of sorts on their own, by disrupting the lives of the locals. Yona felt exactly like her fellow Jungle travellers did. She wanted to forget the discomfort of thinking about that Unda child, so with the help of alcohol she erased the day's events from her mind. At the bar, Yona and her fellow travellers reflected on the simplicity of their identities here: they were just tourists.

'Hey, at first glance, doesn't this place look like Khaosan or De Tham Street?' the writer asked his travel mates. 'The famous tourist streets in Bangkok and Ho Chi Minh City. You know, Bangkok isn't a city to be lonely in. It's the sort of destination for tourists without any innocence, for people who are really explicit about what they want to do. And then Ho Chi Minh City is a bit more unsophisticated, and haggard, really. And Mui, it's, it's something like ...'

The writer went on to a different tourist destination without bothering to describe Mui. Yona felt queasy. She kept thinking about what would complete the writer's sentence: 'Mui, it's, it's something like ...'

The group got more drunk. Yona looked over at the entrance to the bar. The building opened on to a view of sea, or maybe the sea opened on to the building. There was nothing about the opening that you could call a door (or maybe the door was open so wide that Yona couldn't see it). All Yona saw was a plaque hanging above the opening, bearing a sentence that apparently indicated the theme of this place. According to the guide, the sentence meant, 'Drinking is happiness'.

A crowd of local teenagers unfolded music stands in the alley and began to perform. Now the only people outside were Yona and her group. Violin, guitar, drum – the performers played a pleasant melody, the noises cacophonously jumbling together on the street. The whole act charmed Yona: the smiles that showed these teenagers were happy to have listeners, smiles that showed they were bursting with happiness as they performed here, their giggles and then moments of seriousness. Even the teacher's daughter, always distracted, was now a serious listener.

After the performance ended, the teacher walked up to the front and asked the musicians a question.

'What's the name of your band?'

'Thank you teacher,' the teens replied.

It wasn't clear if that was the name of the band or an expression of gratefulness, but anyhow, it was refreshing to see joy among the ruins of Mui. After Thank You Teacher finished their songs, an elderly man dragged his body to the front of the small crowd and began to play the accordion. His legs curled backwards like a merman, and his hat sat open on his knees. Yona found it exciting to watch the accordion expand, making space as it produced sound. According to the guide, this man had been one of the youngest people on Mui during the head-hunting incident, and now he was one of the oldest survivors to remember such events. During the long decades since the massacre, the man's body still hadn't recovered. The old performer who'd lost the use of his legs played his instrument so resonantly that it made the six onlookers reflect once more on why they were there. Yona couldn't point her camera at him. She just stood and listened to the melody as the accordion expanded and contracted.

Someone, probably a local, offered to take a picture of Yona's group. Yona's camera had now recorded the final items on this trip's itinerary: today's activities. She pressed the replay button on her camera and looked at the last picture she'd taken. The camera had a total of six hundred photos, and Yona began to peruse them one by one. But as soon as she saw the Unda child riding on a plastic washbasin, she immediately pressed the delete button.

3

The Cut-off Train Car

–

THE DAY AFTER CHEERING HERSELF UP with alcohol, Yona overslept. She missed breakfast for the first time since arriving in Mui. The group had agreed to meet in the lobby at 10 a.m., and it was already 9.40. Yona felt like throwing up. The ominousness of last night's dream lingered, even if she'd forgotten the plot while washing her face. Maybe she'd dreamed about returning to Seoul. It was the sixth morning of the trip, and today they were heading back. Just like on their way here, the travellers would be going through the airport in Vietnam. According to the schedule, they'd be boarding in the late afternoon, and in the evening they'd touch down at Incheon Airport.

At 9.50, Yona called the front desk and asked for assistance with her luggage. Five minutes later, an employee wearing a loose-fitting uniform drove up in a golf cart. The slim but sturdy man loaded Yona's suitcase and small bag on to his vehicle. It was just like the day she'd arrived. During her stay here, every time Yona requested something from the front desk, this man appeared. Only when it was time to leave did she read his name. A gleaming tag with the name 'Luck' written on it was pinned to his chest.

'Was it a good trip?' Luck asked.

'Yeah, I learned a lot,' Yona replied.

'Well, have a safe trip back.'

All Yona had in her wallet was a few hundred-dollar bills. She noticed that she was carrying a single two-dollar note as well, but that wasn't money she'd intended to use. It was a lucky two-dollar bill someone had given her long ago as a present. Finally Yona pulled it out of her wallet.

'Luck, these two dollars are lucky,' she said. 'If you carry this bill around with you, you'll have good fortune.'

Luck smiled when he saw the money.

The travellers left Mui. Their return route was a little different from the one they'd taken to get here. Now they were going by train rather than by bus. The train from the coast headed towards Ho Chi Minh City's airport; this time, the journey was slightly faster. Everyone in the group sank into their seats and slept or sat quietly. They wouldn't arrive for two more hours, but Yona couldn't stand how uncomfortable her insides felt. She'd drunk too much last night. She felt nauseous, and her stomach gurgled. She walked to the bathroom at the end of the corridor, but even after twenty minutes of waiting, it was still in use.

When she knocked on the door, she could clearly hear a tapping noise coming from inside. Finally she decided to find a bathroom in another car. Placing one hand on her chest and another on the tops of the seats, she tottered forward.

There wasn't a toilet in every train car, so she had to walk for a while before she came across an empty bathroom. Had she ever appreciated a toilet this much? Yona flopped to the ground and almost hugged the porcelain. It had taken her thirty minutes to find and use the facilities. Everything changed in those thirty minutes. Eventually Yona began to walk back in the direction she'd come from. The train wobbled from side to side as always, but something seemed different. The train was now shorter than the distance Yona had walked to reach the bathroom.

At some point in the past thirty minutes, the train had divided into two parts, like those flatworms that could regenerate after being cut in half. Yona realised that now there were only five cars. The bathroom had been in car two, and her original seat in car seven. When she opened the door at the end of the fifth car, she saw only empty tracks following the train like a long tail.

Yona's seat must have been in the part of the train that was cut off. She vaguely remembered an announcement that the train was splitting into two different routes. The problem was that Yona was now on one of the routes, and her bags and fellow travellers were on the other. The two halves of the train were long separated. It had originally been an express train, but now Yona's half was making local stops. Yona needed to know what direction this half was going, but she had no way to find out. Someone who looked like a train employee came up to Yona and asked for a ticket. After looking at Yona's, she shook her head.

'Can't I stay on the train?' Yona asked. 'I need to go to the airport! My luggage and group are all in the other cars – what should I do?'

Yona said it once in Korean and twice in English, but the employee didn't understand. Even so, she comprehended the situation and explained something energetically in the local language.

'Two stops ago, the car you were supposed to be on shifted on to different tracks. That train's an express. You won't reach your destination on this local track. There are no more trains heading in your direction today. If you want to get to the airport, you'll need to look into other forms of transportation. This seat's not available any more.'

Yona couldn't understand the words, but she managed to catch a few things from the woman's gestures and the atmosphere. Your seat's not here; please get off.

The train soon reached the next station, and when the doors opened, Yona was the only person to step out.

She was incredibly lucky to at least have her handbag on her. Yona took out her mobile phone and dialled the guide's number. As soon as the call connected, Lou burst into a fit of anger.

'Where are you?'

Lou's aggressive tone of voice shook Yona. The situation was urgent, but Yona hesitated before answering: 'I went to the bathroom, and then the train ...'

'Ms Ko, I told you on the first day. The train splits in two during the ride, and sometimes the two halves end up going in different directions. That's why I told you only to use the bathroom in your car. I warned you. Do you realise how much we've been looking for you? And do you know when the plane leaves? Get to the airport now, whatever it takes. Where are you?'

'I don't know what the name of this place is. It seems like the sign is in the local language, but I can't read it.'

'Take a taxi or something. Take anything, just make it to the airport in time. If people don't understand you, you have our trip's brochure. The thing that Jungle handed out. If you look at the back cover, there's a map. Point to the airport on the map. Are you listening?'

Yona felt sorry for underestimating Lou. Lou was a competent guide. And right now, Yona was an incompetent traveller. The brochure was sitting inside her suitcase, and the suitcase lay on top of seat twelve in car seven.

'That booklet with the map on it, it's inside my suitcase,' Yona said. 'You know what my suitcase looks like, Lou. I'm sorry.'

'Then grab a taxi, quick. I'll explain where you need to go. Hand the driver the phone.'

Holding her mobile phone in her hand, Yona tried to hail a taxi, but her call had already disconnected.

She put the phone in her bag. She tried to pull out her wallet but couldn't find it. Yona's wallet was packed inside a small pouch along with her passport, but they had both disappeared. Everything Yona needed now was gone. She felt like a child had crawled inside her head, a child who made a mess out of exactly what his mother had just tidied. If you thought about it, everything had gone to ruins. Yona hadn't left her passport in the hotel, had she? Otherwise the resort would have contacted the guide. When Yona and the others got on the bus leaving Mui, Lou had checked all their passports. Yona definitely had her passport then, because that was why she could board the bus – so did Lou have it now? Yona pulled her phone out and called the guide again. She'd been worried for a while about the fact that her phone battery had only one bar left, and the moment the call connected, the phone began to beep. A low battery warning sound.

'Lou, is my passport with you?'

All Yona could hear on the other side was a deep breath.

'Yona. Money – do you have money?'

'I don't even have my wallet. I have some cash that I was carrying separately, but it's not much. What should I do? It seems like people don't really understand English here.'

'Well, first we have to go through the necessary procedures. I'll contact the manager. Since you don't have your passport, even if you make it to the airport, you won't be able to do anything. You'll have to join us later. So, Yona—'

Yona held the suddenly silent phone and sunk to the ground. It wasn't that she'd never travelled, or that she'd never been pickpocketed, or that she'd never forgotten something at a hotel, but this current situation was all too unfamiliar. It was probably because of the language barrier. Yona couldn't read any of the place names here, or understand them if people said the names aloud. No one understood what Yona said, either. She saw a bus in the distance, labelled with the route name 'Gyeongbok-gung to Mapo'. One of the fake Korean routes that the guide had mentioned at some point. The bus drove away without coming closer.

Yona recalled the website that had predicted the day of her death. No matter how much time she had at the beginning, eventually her remaining lifespan would dwindle to nothing. Now Yona had lost another hour's worth of life.

'Ask Paul about the way.'

As soon as Yona read the message, her phone died. It seemed like it had turned off for good this time. Yona tried to find a train station employee, but all she saw were passers-by. A tourist information kiosk was too much to hope for here. This was just a station that she was supposed to have passed through. Even if she tried to talk to someone on the street, the person wouldn't speak Korean or English. No one was selling tickets here, so Yona couldn't just awkwardly stand on the platform waiting for help. Yona realised that she didn't have much travel experience in countries where she didn't speak the language. The places she'd been to before were destinations where she could at least use simple tourist English. Of course, even if the language here was unfamiliar, conversations on buses and in train stations kept to a certain script. Most of them went something like this: 'Would you like a one-way or round trip ticket? Just one?' But this was the first time Yona had been somewhere she couldn't communicate at all. Yona regretted that she hadn't learned any Vietnamese, that she'd left the guidebook with simple Vietnamese phrases in her suitcase. The few words of Vietnamese that Yona did know were only used in happy situations, so in urgent times like this, they'd be as useless as a bounced cheque.

Thankfully, someone at least understood the word 'hotel'. Yona walked down a few blocks as the stranger had directed and entered an alley lined with buildings that must have been hotels, even if they didn't really look like them. It had only been a few hours since she'd left the train, but it felt like days had passed. Standing at the end of the alley, Yona looked up at the sky. She couldn't see the sun, and she felt a little nauseous. Only after poking her head into the first eight hotels lining the street did she find an English speaker, on her ninth try.

'Do you by any chance know someone named Paul?' she asked.

The hotel employee roundly pursed his lips and repeated 'Pa-aul?' back to Yona several times. He asked Yona who Paul was, but Yona obviously didn't know, either. Then she remembered that the guide had said she would contact Belle Époque's manager. When Yona asked the employee to help her get back to Mui, he seemed confused. 'You need to go to Mui?' he asked.

'Yes, Mui. I'm trying to get to the Belle Époque resort there, and I was told to ask Paul for directions. So, um, can I use your phone? I just need to call one person.'

Even though she assumed that her group's plane had already left the airport in Ho Chi Minh City, Yona wanted to double-check. The hotel employee let Yona make a call, but the guide's phone was turned off. She must have already boarded the plane. The man looked at Yona.

'I don't know Paul,' he said, 'but I do know the way back to Mui. You have to go to the port first. Not from this train station, though. Get on a train here and then transfer at the next stop. But there's probably not much time before the last boat leaves.'

Eventually the helpful man decided to take Yona to the dock himself. He hurried outside like it was his job to solve Yona's problems, and it didn't matter if the front desk remained empty. Yona boarded his motor-cycle and put her arms around the man's waist. It was a blessing that she'd lost her suitcase, she thought. The man's motorcycle plunged into an enormous crowd of similar vehicles. Yona covered her ears and nose tightly to protect them from the dust clouds and the din. The hotel employee chattered on like he didn't care if she was listening. He claimed that he could determine if two people riding a motorcycle together were dating, married or just friends, based on their posture.

'Considering the way you're sitting right now, you'd be ...'

After passing through a long tunnel of jarring noises, the man starting speaking again.

'You're sitting like a piece of luggage. So you're not really a rider, you're more like cargo.'

Yona didn't understand the difference between lovers and couples and friends and luggage, but she replied, 'I guess that's right.' She tried not to look flustered. This man seemed trustworthy, but even if he wasn't, she had no other options. Yona maintained a calm demeanour as she struggled to touch her body against his as little as possible. But suddenly she was overcome by a desolate feeling, like the clouds of exhaust that surrounded her. The harbour was on a street that took a long time to get to by motorcycle, and only after reaching the harbour did Yona's surroundings grow familiar. She recognised Phan Thiet. There was the large supermarket in the distance, where they'd bought toothbrushes and coffee on the first day of the trip. Like most people who didn't come across tourists frequently, the man on the motorcycle seemed to feel a combination of curiosity about Yona and responsibility for her. With his guidance, Yona made it to the harbour before the last boat, easily bought a ticket and finally met Paul.

As it turned out, Paul wasn't a person; it was the name of a shipping company. Every boat travelling between Vietnamese coastal cities and Mui belonged to Paul. Yona's body weakened when she learned this. She couldn't tell if she was disheartened or reassured.

A bout of rain noisily erupted over the harbour, and scores of raindrops fell on to the deck. Yona had of course ridden this boat in this direction five nights and six days ago, but now that she was alone, it felt unfamiliar. There weren't many other passengers. A few of them sat in a damp, dark corner of the vessel and stared intensely at Yona.

It was 9 p.m. when they arrived in Mui, but no one was out on the pier. Thankfully, a Paul employee heard Yona say the words 'Belle Époque' and called the resort for her. A car soon arrived at the port. As soon as she saw Belle Époque's logo drawn on the car, Yona filled with relief. She felt further from Korea than ever, but at least there was one familiar place in this foreign land: the resort she'd stayed at a few days ago.

At Belle Époque, though, no one had heard about Yona's situation.

'Did no one contact you?' she asked.

When Yona enquired if they'd got a call from the guide, the manager pulled a strange face. He flipped through a few documents, called someone, and said 'Okay' as he hung up the phone.

'Neither your guide nor the travel company is picking up. Business hours are over for the day,' he told Yona.

'The guide's on the plane, too.'

'Can you give me your passport in the meantime?

I'll let you stay in the bungalow where you were before, for one more night. Tomorrow we'll contact your travel company.'

Yona considered for a moment whether she should tell him that she'd lost her wallet. Tomorrow, they'd probably be able to contact Jungle, and then she could pay for her stay at checkout time. But what if they couldn't get in touch then, either? The next day was Sunday, and in Korea, it was already tomorrow. What if no one answered Jungle's emergency number?

'My passport and wallet were pickpocketed,' Yona blurted out. 'In the train. So my guide told me to come here. I thought she'd told you this.'

'If you don't even have your passport, the situation will be difficult for us.'

The manager spoke without losing his affable smile.

'Who should I contact? There's not a Korean embassy here.'

'Well, in the meantime, stay in the bungalow. It's late and you need to sleep, so we'll make sure you can spend another night here. And I'll contact people in the morning, whether at Jungle or an embassy somewhere. Even though it's the weekend, they have emergency lines. You just need to sleep. But don't go outside, please – I'm breaking policy ...'

Yona got into a golf cart and was driven back to her bungalow. The eyelids by the front door were raised. After Yona went inside, the eyelids lowered again. The room was the same as before, but she didn't feel any of its former cosiness. She perched on the edge of the king-sized bed.

The days Yona loved the most on trips were the unexpected ones. The days that weren't planned, that weren't on the itinerary. Like if she stayed an extra night, or decided to do something spontaneous. Sometimes, when Yona was presented with an unexpected twenty-four hours, she'd return home at the end of the trip and only remember that one break in her schedule. Days like this couldn't be insignificant, but neither could they pull Yona away from the rhythm of ordinary life. Today had been too painful to be a welcome break. Yona realised how hungry she was. It seemed awkward to notice hunger in a situation like this, but her stomach's emptiness was exacerbating her fear. On the table, Yona saw a gift bag filled with fruit, with a cereal bar and chocolate nearby. Who had set those out, knowing beforehand that someone would stay here tonight? Had someone prepared the snacks during the brief interval Yona was away from the resort? Yona debated whether she should take one, before ripping open the packaging on the multigrain cereal bar. She put the bar in her mouth and mindlessly chewed. Just the act of cutting into something with her teeth seemed to prove that she wasn't dreaming. She tried to bite the inside of her cheek to feel some sort of pain, but for some reason the pink flesh wasn't easy to grab hold of.

In the morning, as soon as she opened her eyes, the enormous ceiling fan came into view. At some point in the past, when visiting the Leeum Art Museum, Yona had laid down beneath the statue *Maman* by

Louise Bourgeois. Then, it was just to snap a photo, but this morning she felt like she was lying under that spider sculpture again. This time, not to take a picture, but to be eaten. Yona sat up abruptly.

Her mobile phone was useless. The dead phone was now in as dire straits as she was. Yona walked towards the lobby, but she knew she shouldn't enter the resort's dining hall. When she'd travelled from her bungalow to the main building by golf cart, the distance had felt very short, but now that she was walking, it was far. The route differed slightly by foot, too. Yona didn't see a single person until she reached the lobby; perhaps none of the gardeners worked on Sunday. The resort seemed frozen, and she wondered for the first time if this whole situation had been somehow staged. Then the manager approached, and summed up her predicament all too clearly.

'Ms Ko, there haven't been any calls from the travel company, and no one picks up when we try to contact them. What would you like us to do?'

Yona dialled the numbers to Jungle's emergency phone number, but the call cut off after three rings. None of the company's employees had been in a crisis like this while travelling for work. Yona's situation wasn't going to be recorded as an accident; they'd think it was carelessness. She was just going to have to wait until Lou returned and sorted everything out. Waiting to be a Jungle customer once more, waiting to be saved: that seemed like Yona's safest option.

Yona pulled her camera out of her bag.

'If you hold on to this, can I stay for one more night? Today's Sunday, so just one night longer.'

The manager thought about it for a moment and then accepted the camera, saying that he'd allow another twenty-four hours, no more.

'You must be hungry. I'll make you a simple breakfast, since the dining hall is closed today.'

Yona ate pancakes the manager prepared for her. So this is my situation now, she thought as she dropped on to the sofa in her room, relieved but exhausted. She picked up the remote and pressed its buttons repeatedly like the teacher's six-year-old daughter. The eyelid-shaped signals on the front of the bungalow opened and closed over and over. Then Yona walked on to the beach and wandered to the back of the resort. Thick electrical wires hung between telephone poles, between awnings and fences. The wires looked like horizontal lines on a page of sheet music. Several birds descended like musical notes, and the ends of the wires rolled up into a tangle resembling a treble clef. Yona must have seen this all before, but several days ago she hadn't had the time for such scenery. Signs of life only now came into view, and those unfamiliar shapes moving around Yona actually made the whole area feel more familiar.

After walking a while, Yona spotted the sign for 'Mui Market', but she didn't see a single tent or street stall. She passed the Mui Market sign and continued. Soon she was once again in an unfamiliar environment.

The Sunday morning alley was still asleep. Yona peered at a house. Among the broken fences and shattered windows, someone was looking out through the cracked glass. The moment Yona became aware of the person's gaze, it disappeared. This must have been her first time on this road, but it didn't feel new. She felt like she recognised the graffiti on the walls and remembered snapping a picture of the nonsensical Korean slogan that was written there because she thought it was funny. She wasn't in an unknown place after all; instead, she was looking at an already-familiar path in a new way. In just two days, the structures around her looked like they'd been jumbled up. It didn't look the same, and seemed to have somehow grown larger than before.

Yona saw someone in the distance and approached. It was the old man who played the accordion and had lost his legs in the sinkhole. Now he stood upright, on what looked like his own two legs, playing golf with a broom and bits of scrunched up paper. He was so intent upon getting the paper into round holes in the ground that he didn't notice Yona coming over.

'What are you doing here?'

Yona was the one to ask the question, but the situation seemed to call for an answer from her, too. She continued to speak as she pulled the straps of her bag towards her body.

'I'm just on a walk. But what are you doing?'

The old man glanced at Yona and then lowered his head towards the ground again. He was standing – and with such straight posture. Did this mean his earlier appearance had been a show? Yona called out to the old man again. He stared back at her and for a moment he seemed to be hesitating, but then he continued with his game of golf. Yona welled with fury. The man looked angry, too, maybe angrier than Yona. He hurled the broom in her direction and sat down on a tree stump.

'Please,' he said. 'We need time off, too.'

By the time the old man had finished his sentence, Yona had already left the alley in a rush. Mui was not the place she thought it was. What Yona had seen during her Jungle trip was simple, unsophisticated countryside devastated by an old disaster, where 'one dollar' was the most popular phrase among locals. But the Mui she was walking around now felt like a theme park that wasn't yet open. The old man hadn't exactly felt threatening, but goosebumps dotted Yona's arms. She turned towards the path she'd come from and began to walk. Her pace quickened.

Yona saw a house with the door open in front of her. She walked towards it. Inside, a woman was watching television. She stood up when she realised a person was nearby and turned around, shrieking at the sight of Yona.

'Do you have a reason to be here?' asked the woman.

'I'm looking for the way to the resort. I'm lost.'

'Belle Époque?'

'Yes.'

The woman turned off the television and went outside.

'Go straight, and when you see a forked path, turn left. You'll see the ocean, and if you follow the shore, you'll get to the back gate of the resort.'

Yona was surprised by the woman's English. Her voice sounded familiar. When she spoke, her mouth contorted into familiar shapes as well. As Yona began to recognise the woman, the woman seemed to recognise Yona a little bit, too. The woman crossed her arms and walked back through the door to her house, hunching a little bit. Yona had seen that action before.

'Hey! Have we met?' Yona asked.

The woman looked like she was about to say something, but kept her mouth shut and just smiled timidly. She was definitely Nam. The woman who'd led Yona and the other travellers around during the one-night homestay.

'Your name was Nam, wasn't it? Hey, look at this!'

Yona outstretched her ten fingers and showed off her pink manicure. But the woman in front of her looked embarrassed, and angry. She rushed back into her house.

'Nam,' Yona called from outside.

The windows of the house next door creaked open and then quietly closed. She couldn't see anyone from where she was, but Yona realised that over the past few minutes, the many eyes in this alley had begun to flicker in her direction.

Yona started down the path Nam had described. She wanted to look back, but it felt like the moment she turned around, she'd transform into a pillar of salt.

The resort looked like a red spot in the distance. But what caught Yona's eye wasn't that spot, it was the road bending left at a forty-five-degree angle. She heard some sort of sound coming from down the road, so she peered cautiously to the side. Then she began to slowly walk down the left edge of the fork. Moments later, a massive truck rushed around the corner at speed, screeching to a halt and throwing something from inside several metres up into the sky. Whatever it was, was shaped like a person. Yona hid behind a tree and clamped her lips shut. Someone hurriedly stepped down from the driver's seat and approached the fallen figure. When the driver saw that the person on the road was still breathing, he got back in his truck. The vehicle reversed, to secure a bit of space, then accelerated fast enough not only to grind the pebbles under its wheels to bits, but also any person who happened to be lying on the ground. Yona knew what the truck had run over without having to look.

The driver stood in front of the body and made a phone call. A few minutes later, a different car arrived and some people got out and collected the body, Yona could see the victim's face. It was the accordion man. His broom lay next to him. Dizziness and fear rose up inside Yona. She closed her eyes and took a deep breath. When she opened them, she saw someone on the road looking in her direction. Yona stepped back. Her right ankle twisted. And then she felt arms around her. She looked up and saw a familiar face.

4

Three Weeks Later

—

'YOU SAID YOU SAW A TRUCK?' the manager asked, as if Yona had told him something strange. His accusatory tone set Yona on edge. She was too scared to tell him that she'd witnessed an accident, too.

'You must not have seen right. Outsiders never see those trucks. That's a rule.'

'It was a yellow truck.'

'Well, then it belongs to Paul. Those trucks are used for construction, or for public safety. But because of the noise they make, they're not used when outsiders visit.'

'How does Paul know if outsiders are on the island?'

'Because all the visitors stay at this resort. If there are guests here, Paul doesn't use large trucks. Since I registered you, there's a guest on the record at Belle Époque, so Paul's vehicles aren't permitted to drive around. More importantly, though, it seems like we need to have another conversation.'

The manager stared straight at Yona as he spoke.

'I mean about you breaking your promise. I said that you absolutely could not leave the resort gate. What would Jungle say to us if something happened to you? If our employees hadn't found you outside, we would have no idea if you were in trouble.'

'I didn't see a gate. The walking trail by the sea is connected to the village.'

'No it's not. There's a border between the sea and the village. It might not be tall, but there is a fence. If you went out that way, you definitely crossed the resort gate.'

Yona couldn't deny it. The manager held her bill out to her. 'You broke your promise,' he said. He added that he still hadn't been able to contact Jungle. That in this situation, he couldn't help Yona any more. As the manager spoke, wrinkles appeared in the middle of his forehead.

'Since it looks like you won't make it to the boat today, stay here tonight. Tomorrow morning, I'll escort you to the harbour. That's the limit to what we can do for former guests. I don't know if you realise, but if you're not an approved foreigner, you can't just remain in Mui. Especially if you're a foreigner without any identification.'

'Then where do I get approval?'

'From Paul.'

Paul was connected to everything here. Yona repeated the word 'Paul' in her head, until it started to sound like 'foul'. She felt overwhelmed. She couldn't erase the suspicion that she'd fallen into the grips of an organisation as disconcerting as Jungle. Yona decided to call Jungle's emergency number. Her passport and wallet had vanished, and all she had left was a few small coins innocently scattered about her purse pocket: that scared her. The phone connected to Kim more easily than expected, considering that the work day in Korea was already over. But Yona soon regretted that she'd reached him so quickly.

'It was your mistake not returning on schedule,' Kim berated her. 'How can you expect the company to straighten this out for you? You have to get back on your own. You can't just hope that someone else will take care of you. Don't think of your situation as being left behind – why not see it as more like an extension of your trip? You have to turn this into an opportunity. Remember: you haven't got a raise in three years, and that suggests something about your performance. I'm disappointed in you.'

Kim's casual attitude made Yona even more nervous. For a moment, she had forgotten that Jungle mattered more than Mui, that her office could be scarier than this island. She couldn't ask Kim to bring her back to Korea. There had to be another way to leave this place. She could call friends in Korea and ask them to send money to the resort. Then she'd have to ask Belle Époque how to get to Ho Chi Minh City's airport. There were several ways to fix this. Why had she called Jungle and not anyone else? Over the past decade, had Yona become too dependent upon her employer?

Yona had initially applied to work at Jungle because

she liked travel, but after surviving ten years there, the company had begun to mean something else to her. Even if Jungle sold something other than travel, even if Yona actually created something other than trips, she did her job diligently. And now she was thirty-three. Jungle was the ideal company for people who didn't have time for dating outside of work. It encouraged office couples, and it even provided opportunities each weekend for single employees to meet other singles. It also offered nearby employee housing. A doctor's office, theatre, sports centre and shopping mall were all located inside the office. There was just one downside to a company like this. The moment you quit your job, you had to restructure your entire life.

The call hadn't been worth the effort, but that didn't mean it had gone unnoticed. Someone pressed the doorbell to her bungalow, and when she opened the door, a golf cart was waiting outside. It was the manager.

'There's something we need to discuss,' he said. His expression was different from yesterday's.

'I see that you made an international phone call.'

'Yes, bill me for that, too,' Yona replied.

'You called Jungle, didn't you?'

'I did.'

'Why didn't you tell me? That you were a Jungle employee?'

'Do you listen in on guests' phone calls?' Yona responded indignantly. She was shocked by how accusatory the manager was acting.

'It seems like this conversation is going to take a while, so let's go inside and talk. Luck, Mr Hwang is coming. Go show him inside.'

The dark clouds in the sky grew larger, and rain began to splatter on to the ground. Yona followed the manager to his office. He prepared refreshments for them, and his voice softened.

'I want to apologise for what happened yesterday. I'm very sensitive about our visitors here, and I didn't realise you were a Jungle employee. I made a mistake, treating you so harshly.'

The manager handed Yona's camera back to her. He asked for one of her business cards, but of course Yona didn't have her wallet.

'The truth is, I was a bit sensitive because yesterday morning I got a notification from Jungle, saying that they needed further review before renewing our contract. It was a letter, sent by mail. As you know, we can't get in touch with them on the phone.'

'Really? I don't think they're reviewing the contract yet. Jungle isn't going to deal with this resort's programme until I return. Of course, considering the quality of service here, I'm going to tell them we should cut our losses.'

'Can you change the results of the review?' the manager asked.

'Yes, that's why I came here – to look into the package you offer.'

Yona was the person in charge of this case, and her briefing hadn't arrived at Jungle's headquarters yet, so what did it mean that a notification regarding contract renewal had already been mailed to the resort? I'm supposed to be the only Jungle employee in contact with Belle Époque, Yona thought to herself. To think that the resort was getting mail from Jungle that she knew nothing about. Yona struggled to conceal her anxious expression. She sat upright, wavering slightly.

'I realise that some of my actions were a breach of etiquette. But I'm begging you,' the manager implored. 'You can't abandon us now. There's still a lot for you to see here.'

The manager's pleas echoed Yona's imagined pleas to Jungle. *I dedicated so much of my time to the company, giving up weekends and working while buried deep in shame – and now you want to get rid of me?*

'The rating I'm giving Mui is a D. Usually, Jungle renews the contracts rated B or higher. Of course, a D has more room for re-evaluation than an E or F does.'

As they came out of her mouth, the sentences made Yona uncomfortable. She felt empathy for this D-rated programme.

'So it's not completely out of the running,' the manager responded. 'Why do you think Mui is a D?'

'Jungle offers about one hundred and fifty differ-ent travel packages. Programmers are constantly designing trips, so a package has to be powerful to survive. We've got earthquakes, typhoons, volcanoes, avalanches, droughts, floods, fires, massacres, wars, radioactivity, desertification, serial killers, tsunamis, animal abuse, contagious diseases, water pollution, asylums, prisons and more. The packages Koreans like are those with something exotic, the spirit of adventure. But there's nothing like that on Mui. Head-hunting and a sinkhole opening up in the ground are appealing premises, but the problem is that they happened fifty years ago. Also, it's hard to call the desert here a desert. It's really more of a dune. And the homestay at the house on stilts, well ... that kind of attraction could be recreated at any old museum or theme park, so it just felt like fluff. Mui is appealing in that it's an unknown place, like any foreign country. But it doesn't really seem like a disaster destination you'd pay money to visit, does it?'

'It was very popular at the beginning.'

'Its time has run out. If a destination doesn't have enough tourist attractions to keep it going, it's kicked off the roster.'

They heard a knocking sound, and the manager got up from his seat.

'It looks like Mr Hwang has arrived. This is someone you'll know.'

The door opened, and the writer from the Jungle trip, Junmo Hwang, entered the room. As soon as he saw Yona, he opened his mouth in surprise.

'It's you! Someone told me there was another Korean here, but I didn't realise it was you, Yona. Hey, why have you got so thin over the past few days? Have you not returned to Korea yet, or did you leave and come back again?'

Yona gasped upon seeing the writer. 'I haven't been able to leave yet,' she replied. 'Why are you here again?'

Only a few days had passed since the two had

parted, but the writer looked incredibly happy, as if they hadn't seen each other for a very long time. Raindrops hit the window with increasing strength. The manager brought out coffee with evaporated milk and macaroons.

'Sit down and let's talk. We have a lot to discuss, so make yourself comfortable.'

The writer downed half his coffee in one gulp.

'Oh my gosh, our guide was about to explode when we realised you were gone. We were considering missing our flight and getting a later one. Everyone in the group wanted you to come back with us, so we waited. But we couldn't contact you, so finally we just got on the next plane. And that kid wouldn't stop crying the entire flight. Something about leaving her sketchbook behind.'

'Did you come to retrieve me?' Yona asked.

'If that were the case, I would be honoured,' the writer said in jest.

Feigning disappointment that he couldn't play the role of Yona's saviour, the writer inhaled deeply and drank the rest of the coffee.

'I came for work. I told you about the various side gigs that help me earn a living, didn't I? I'm a freelancer; during our trip, I worked for Jungle, and now I'm working here. I'll be in Mui until my contract expires.'

'You worked for Jungle?'

'Yeah, it was a temporary gig. That trip originally needed at least five people to depart, but because there were only four, I was hired to fill in. The idea was that I'd be a monitor. Anyway, I met a beautiful lady like you, Yona, so it wasn't bad at all. Ha ha.'

'I work for Jungle, too.'

'Really?'

'I'm a full-time employee.'

'Huh, you're a cut above me, then. Were you doing some sort of secret job? And what kind of Jungle employee gets marooned like this?'

Yona shrugged her shoulders to show that she didn't know. The writer told her that her suitcase was currently in a storage box at the airport in Ho Chi Minh City. He also let her charge her phone, which had been dead for the past few days. When the phone turned on, Yona realised that the text urging her to 'ask Paul' didn't come from the guide's number. 'Ask Paul the way, and find beautiful ladies in your area' was the whole text. Yona felt drained.

This spam text that had followed her all the way to a foreign country made Yona's head hurt. She thought about how she'd ended up in such a preposterous place. But hadn't the guide definitely mentioned the manager? That's what she remembered. Had she failed to understand something else? Maybe this entire situation was the finale to a yellow card designed to test her. The current trial she was undergoing? Maybe it was part of the work trip she'd been sent on. Yona recalled how Kim had told her she needed to find the way back herself. She wondered if the debacle she'd fallen into was a disaster, or the chaos that lay beyond disasters. She couldn't stop thinking about it; somehow, the more she entertained doubts about what was going on, the deeper she seemed to be falling into a swamp. Now, ironically, when Yona couldn't trust Jungle, the resort trusted Yona. Precisely because Yona worked for Jungle.

'But what kind of job are you doing here, Junmo?' Yona asked.

'First get in the car. There's somewhere we need to go.'

The three of them got in the car and drove down the road that circled Mui. The writer whispered something into Yona's ear. *Don't be surprised.*

The car stopped in front of the red sand desert. It wasn't far from the white sand desert, but the land here gave off an entirely different energy. For a start, the whole place resembled a construction site. In front of them was a wall, three metres tall, that seemed to encircle the entire red desert area, and all they could see above the wall was the incomplete tower, soaring upwards. A tower that, according to plan, would become a lookout point where you could take in both the desert and the ocean at once. But since construction was suspended a year ago, everything had stopped. Even if the company in charge did finish erecting the tower, the structure was sure to eat up money, so they were leaving it alone for now. The tower mimicked the form of a human body, and inside it a spiral staircase leading to the lookout had been installed. But it had no real features above the neck. At first the sculpture had been designed in Jesus' image, then the current company had taken charge of the project and turned it into a Mary statue. But now it had no face at all.

The writer stared at up the expressionless mass and asked, 'If I do my job well, will they carve my face up there?'

The manager answered, smiling.

'Construction on the tower is going to begin again. Paul started resolving things about six months ago, and they've decided to finish the task. Did you guys know that our resort is affiliated with Paul, too?'

Yona lightly shook her head.

'The truth is, two construction firms already pulled out because they thought the project was a money pit. But now that Paul has invested, it's obvious that things are turning around. Paul has invested a significant amount of money in Mui.'

Yona had loosely assumed that Paul was just a shipping company. She still didn't know anything about Paul. But she didn't want to reveal her ignorance, so she asked about the business indirectly.

'What do you think about Paul?'

'Well … it's a skilful company,' the manager replied, like there was an obvious correct answer.

'Is that right?'

'Paul doesn't stick its hands into ventures that are going to fail,' the manager added.

Your resort is so dead that flies are buzzing around it, Yona thought to herself.

'We have to save Mui, if only to avoid disappointing Paul. That's how Belle Époque will survive, too. If Paul pulls out of Mui, the real disaster begins.'

They entered the humanoid tower through its feet. The narrow spiral staircase rose up in front of them. The manager led the way, and his voice rang out between the rounded steps.

'Do you know why Paul invested in Mui?'

'Uh ...' Yona didn't know what to say.

'Because it's cheap. Right now, everything in Mui is available at rock-bottom prices. Especially if you compare it with other countries in the region. Paul bought Mui's potential, and for hardly any money at all. If you think about it, this is an opportunity for Jungle, too. Mui is so low, all it can do now is rise back up.'

Yona listened without talking. Every time the group completed one rotation of stairs, a round window appeared in the wall, and if not for those windows, it would have felt like the structure was suffocating them. The writer grumbled that they'd barely reached the sculpture's knees. This wasn't his first time here; he'd already visited three times. If you entered on the opposite side, an lift went up to the lookout point, but the lift wasn't working.

'Paul is going to succeed in its investment,' the manager continued. 'According to what I've heard, international organisations are soon going to launch a disaster recovery programme in this area. The organisations will pick one of the region's disaster zones and donate an enormous amount of money for urban redevelopment. For sewage repairs, problems with electricity, road maintenance, even people's jobs: everything.

A window hadn't appeared for a very long time.

'If all of that is true, do you think that Mui would be selected for such a programme?' Yona asked.

'We have to make sure it is,' the manager said.

Because there were no more windows, it felt like they were continuously revolving around the same spot, and motion sickness welled up inside Yona's stomach.

'Isn't it possible that Paul's investment could lead to nothing? If disaster doesn't hit Mui, it won't be a candidate for a recovery programme. And you can't hope Mui will fall into ruins for specifically this reason. The timing of disasters isn't something humans decide.'

'Well, timing is the easy part.'

Now the manager was addressing the writer.

'Mui suffered from a drought all spring. Once the wet season began, rain started to fall in torrents. Sinkholes occur in areas where the ground is weak, especially when there's heavy rain to set them off. Our timing's okay.'

Yona wondered what he meant about timing. The writer strode ahead of the manager and opened the door at the top of the steps. Finally they'd reached the tower's neck and could look out. Wind mixed with crunchy flecks of sand rushed into the formerly enclosed space. Far off, they caught sight of the ocean surrounding them, throwing its blue undulations at the wind. Between the water and this tower lay the red sand desert, which resembled a golf course. The sand in the middle of the desert sank down into two rounded holes. The sight shocked Yona. They looked exactly like sinkholes.

The hole on the right side was close to a perfect circle, nearly as expansive as the head lake. The one on the left was slightly smaller, but it looked deep. Yona had never witnessed sinkholes this big, not even in photos, and especially not two that had occurred right next to each other. And right in the middle of the desert? She was surprised, too, by how sturdy the walls of the holes looked. Maybe it was because she was looking down from a distance. Perhaps if she got a closer view, she'd see sand plummeting inside.

'When did this happen? This incident – or did ... ?'

'Or what?'

Or, was something else going on? This place still seemed like a construction site. At the edge of the desert, a large digger was parked. It was frozen, its long neck stooped, like an animal so thin its bones were exposed. And what was the wall surrounding the desert for? Yona wondered if it was protecting – or hiding – something other than this incomplete tower. She looked down at the two grave-like valleys: they looked like the site of the head hunting from fifty years earlier. The nearby sand's reddish hue gave the area even more of a murderous atmosphere. The holes were so deep, the desert sandstorms probably couldn't even reach them. It was the same up here, on the tower. This vertical structure successfully avoided the horizontally blowing wind. Yona rubbed her arms.

The writer began to tell Yona a story that reminded her of the children's game 'If You Go to Market'. You just had to change 'market' for 'desert'. If you go to the desert, there is fruit; if you go to the desert, there is fruit and bread; if you go to the desert, there is fruit and bread and tents; if you go to the desert, there is fruit and bread and tents and wheelbarrows; if you go to the desert, there is fruit and bread and tents and wheelbarrows and fathers; if you go to the desert, there is fruit and bread and tents and wheelbarrows and fathers and sons – and so forth. As long as no one forgot a word, the game could continue forever. The writer explained that the desert would be filled with a similarly endless number of items three weeks from now, on the first Sunday of August: the field day for Mui's only elementary school, to be followed by the village festival in the afternoon. From early morning, vehicles and people carrying food would descend upon the red sand desert. At 9 a.m. field day would commence among the dunes. After avoiding the sun for a bit at lunchtime, villagers would begin the festival at 3 p.m. But instead of this schedule, what would actually happen was that at 8 a.m., the ground would begin to crumble, and the first sinkhole would appear. And before the people of Mui could straighten things out, the second hole would open up. Twenty cars and motorcycles would be sucked into the two holes, along with one hundred citizens.

The writer explained that the first sinkhole was located in a spot where, two days before the festival, locals would discover a puddle two metres in diameter and one metre deep, the sand hollowed out like someone had excavated the desert with an ice cream scoop. Such puddles appeared every so often. The desert sometimes revealed osteoporosis-like pockets of emptiness. But this time, people would be surprised by the puddle's size. It was a lot bigger than earlier puddles, big enough to cause an accident. And because the puddle was situated right below the tower, in the middle of the desert, they couldn't just install a safety fence around it. Two days before the event, the school would fill the hole and place various adornments over it: emergency first aid so people couldn't walk over the wound in the ground. But then it would collapse, one hour before the event. What was initially two metres in diameter would spread to almost forty metres, with a depth close to sixty. Soon after the first sinkhole, the second sinkhole would appear nearby. Right below where most of the festival organisers were standing, and without warning.

'The second sinkhole will be almost thirty metres in diameter and at least two hundred metres deep,' the writer explained. 'That's where most of the casualties will be. Almost all of them, in fact.'

Yona descended the tower's stairs in a stupor, feeling like she had stepped into some kind of night-mare. In the car on the way back to the resort, she was silent. When she did start asking questions back in the manager's office, the writer didn't answer any of them, but he did hand her several photos.

'This is a diamond mine in South America,' he said. 'In 1871, diamonds were discovered on a hill there, and people flocked to the area. Within a few months, they'd dug a cave one hundred metres deep. Of course, their goal wasn't to create a sinkhole, but that's what happened naturally. They had almost thirty thousand people digging for diamonds. We just have twenty.'

'Does – does that mean *you* made those holes in the desert?' Yona asked.

'Well, those twenty workers drove the diggers and carried the shovels, of course, not me personally.'

The writer showed Yona a few more pictures. They were photos he'd taken earlier, of the sinkhole construction site, and the workers operating the machinery digging the holes. Like the Sarisariñama sinkhole in Venezuela, the sinkholes consisted initially of small divots appearing one after another, resembling dens for underground animals. At some point, these tiny openings merged into two enormous holes: the shapes Yona had just witnessed.

'But why?' Yona asked. 'Why did you dig those holes? And what was the story you just told me about what's going to happen there?'

The writer sighed.

'Yona, you haven't been listening. This is very important, pay attention. Three weeks from now, it will be the first Sunday of August. We've prepared the sinkholes, and on that day we'll reveal them. Everything's going to happen just like in the story you just heard.'

The manager lit a cigarette. He blew out his smoke away from Yona.

'What do you think?' he asked. 'Will this incident be suitable for a new Jungle trip?'

The wind changed direction, and the manager's smoke blew in Yona's face.

'So, logically, what you're saying means—'

'Logically, Mui can't wait any longer. There's not really a difference between dying in a natural disaster and starving to death, is there? In the current situation, dying in a natural disaster would be preferable. Since signing a contract with Jungle and building the resort, Mui has been tailoring everyday life to fit its role as a disaster zone. That's led young workers who left for other regions to come back. Now, if disaster disappears from Mui, life disappears, too.'

The manager stamped harder than necessary on the cigarette he'd thrown to the ground.

'You can't disappoint Paul,' he said.

This project had covertly been under way for six months. Visitors were decreasing in number, and the resort had noticed uneasy signs of apathy from Jungle. Now Mui was creating its own story. Yona opened and shut her mouth, fumbling for words. She had to propose an alternative.

'Manager, have you heard of Pai?' she asked. 'What about you, Junmo?'

The manager shook his head. The writer didn't know what Pai was, either.

'It's a small village in Thailand. Pai was originally a way station on the way from Chiang Mai to Mae Hong Son, but as travellers began to stay there for longer periods of time, it became the destination it is now.'

'What's there?'

'There's nothing in Pai. If you visit, you'll see a lot of stores selling T-shirts with the sentence "There's nothing to do in Pai" written on them. "There's nothing special about Pai", "Pai: do nothing here": slogans like that. People like those slogans. The whole point is that there's nothing to do. You can feel a sense of peace there. I bought one of the shirts, too. It said "Pai is all right". Wearing that shirt, I spent a somewhat boring week there. But after I came home, I kept think-ing about that somewhat boring week. I still dream about Pai. Most of the tourists who visit the town are entranced by its charm. What if you tried to create an environment like Pai's here?'

'Pai is Pai and Mui is Mui.'

As the manager said that, he got up from his chair and looked out the window. It was quiet. Since things had come to this, Yona couldn't help but ask the ques-tion she'd been trying to avoid.

'How are you going to cause one hundred casualties?'

That was nothing to worry about, they told her.

Some people believe Heinrich's Law: that before a disaster occurs, hundreds of small signs foretell what's about to come. But Heinrich's Law only focuses on the event, not the victims. Those injured in a disas-ter don't have premonitions. To the victims, disasters come quickly. One day, the ground suddenly col-lapses beneath your feet: an incident too jarring to be a coincidence, too sad to be fate. How could one arti-ficially create something like this?

'Before I got this job writing Mui's sinkhole story, I worked as a photographer,' the writer said. 'People are always taking photos of themselves in front of things, but the pictures are never very interesting. So I started to do the opposite, and for money, too. I would look at photos people sent me and recreate the scenes so they were more interesting. Once I got so many online requests, I couldn't sleep for a week. People brought in cameras asking me to recreate their photos, they showed me room interiors to copy; in some cases, I redid graduation photos by casting similar-looking people to stand in for the original subjects. And now I'm working on disasters. The sinkhole's not my first. Disaster and catastrophe aren't just within the realm of the gods. Us humans, we can manipulate nature, too.'

Junmo Hwang had only got this job because there was a demand for disasters. He wouldn't reveal where he'd worked before, but he said no one ever found out that the disaster he'd planned was man-made. Don't believe everything that happens in the world, he warned. Roughly three per cent of it was fake.

'Are you not uneasy about what you're doing?' Yona asked.

'Unease is like a pair of shoes, allowing the artist to go where he needs to go.'

'But after the sinkholes occur, a lot of people will be investigating what caused them.'

'The official cause will be foundation work on the tower. Yona, I'm not an amateur. Sinkholes happen when a layer of underground rock dissolves, or the earth is weak, or due to internal shock from something like an earthquake. They can also appear when groundwater dries up, or the land is parched because of a drought. I've come up with a cause that combines all of these issues. The tower. That tower is going to become our alibi. When construction on the tower began, it overwhelmed the desert. That's what I mean. Even though the holes are man-made, they've grown a whole lot bigger than what we originally dug. Both in diameter and depth. We've been surprised by how smoothly work is progressing. Usually sinkholes happen in areas with a lot of limestone, but whether the ground here is limestone or not, it wasn't that difficult to create the holes. Even if we stopped work on them now, I think they would keep growing. And then there's the tower shooting up over there, looking like it might fall over. You can think of this project as half human, half created by the desert itself.'

Yona thought about how sinkholes can eat up a five-lane road in five minutes. These two holes would swallow an entire village's field day, like an enormous snake gulping down a frog the size of a house. Time was now flowing towards the event, like sewage sucked into a drain. The whirlpool had already begun. Yona had to decide if she was going to join in or run away.

The manager opened a bottle of whisky and filled three glasses. He gazed at Yona's glass and said, 'I want you to help with this project, Yona. Do you know why I'm making you this offer?'

'Well ...'

'It's not just because you're a Jungle employee. Of course it's true that we need travel experts, but that's not all. I'm asking because I was certain that you wouldn't refuse.'

Yona drank a sip of the alcohol to hide her strange sense of displeasure.

'What I mean is, if you'd decided to go back to Korea – if you'd heard our plans and didn't want to be a part of them – you would have left earlier. But you're still here. That makes me trust you. I'm pretty good at judging people.'

'What do you want from me?'

'Don't you have the authority to save Mui? You're the person in charge of contract renewal.'

'You're mistaken to think that the contract will be renewed just because I give the okay. Jungle project organisers don't have absolute power. This programme is going to fail no matter what I do. I'm sorry, but that's the truth.'

'What if there's a new programme?'

'A new programme?'

'After the event occurs in August, we'll start offering a new programme right away. It'll be a complete travel package, set right here in Mui. It doesn't matter whether it's five nights and six days or five nights and seven days. Since you're the expert in that area, I think you can create the perfect package, both for Jungle and for Korean travellers. What do you think about staying here, doing research and coming up with a new itinerary? If you prepare the trip beforehand, it will be good both for you and for your company. Jungle can unveil its new programme immediately after the disaster happens, when the island is still straightening things out. We need to coordinate the timing of our actions, before it's too late.'

'What will I get out of this?' Yona asked.

'You'll have complete authority over this travel package. Our resort will only work with you. This trip will excite your boss, I'm sure of it.'

Yona felt like a small hole had been drilled into her body, and the manager was peeping through the hole and looking at her insides. Yona had lost count of the number of times she'd dedicated months to a single project, only to have it fall apart or be taken away from her. This time, it wouldn't be a bad idea to build up trust with local government officials and the partner hotel to ensure success. And no one would find out about her involvement in the creation of the sinkholes, would they?

At Jungle, the first thing Yona did when she got to work in the morning was determine the location and intensity of disasters that had occurred overnight. She had to sort through newspaper articles, social networking sites, and press releases from international organisations. She'd spent ten years doing this. But during this trip, Yona had begun to feel like she'd lost direction. She grew anxious just thinking about the stories she'd tracked, and couldn't get rid of a lingering attachment to the Jinhae package. Scattered remnants of the city were probably spread across the ocean at this point, ready to be discovered. Yona hadn't left behind a life in Jinhae, but somehow it seemed like fragments of her, too, were strewn across the Pacific.

Yona thought about the employee who had pre-ceded her at Jungle. She'd never seen his face, but she felt like she knew him better than anyone. It was because of the rumours. The man had submitted a res-ignation letter, but with Kim's coercion, he'd decided to take six months off instead; after this person had departed, rumours about him echoed throughout Jungle's office.

'I thought Section Chief Park just kept his head down, but now he's trying to quit.'

'Really? I knew he was a bad seed. When he's upset, he doesn't just do things by half. All or nothing: that's his style.'

Considering that Park had handed in a resigna-tion letter and the boss turned it into a trip, everyone thought that Park had won. But six months later, after he returned from his time off, Section Chief Park got the worst performance reviews in the office, and soon he was transferred to a branch everyone hoped to avoid. After that, Park wrote a real resignation letter. The employees who remained couldn't stop gossiping about him.

'It's a predictable story,' they said. 'After six months off, it's November, almost performance rating season. Team Leader Kim was trying to step all over Park. He needed someone to send to that prison, anyway. When people like Park turn in resignation letters, they're sacrificed for those of us who wouldn't dare quit. I thought it was strange when Team Leader Kim tried to convince him not to resign, but now I realise he was just using Park for his own gain. Isn't he the kind of guy who'd do something like that? He squeezes the juices right out of people.'

Yona was hired to take over Section Chief Park's job, and even though the position had been empty for a long time, hints of her predecessor remained. Here and there, she saw the name Sungdong Park automatically filled in on planning forms, so she had to replace it with her name. She also got frequent calls that came out of nowhere and asked, 'What was Sungdong Park like?' Yona had a hard time grasping the speakers' hidden intentions, or even determining who they were. Maybe these people worked for other companies where Sungdong Park had sent his résumé. Even though she didn't know him, Yona replied like they were old acquaintances and confidently assured the caller that he was a good person.

Yona felt the sudden urge to place a similar call to Jungle, to say, 'Please give me Yona Ko from programme team three.' What kind of answer would she get? Would a replacement already be sitting in her seat?

Yona stared at the transparent glass of whisky placed in front of her and considered what lay behind it. She thought about the meaning of this trip. About the messages she'd got from Jungle, that they were ignoring the person in charge here: her. Yona had to accept it. It looked like Jungle had dealt with her in the same manner as her predecessor. You'd think that when normality unravelled, it did so suddenly, but the truth was that Yona's sinkhole-like collapse resulted from several years of pressure.

'Do you know what real disaster is?' the manager asked Yona.

Yona's fellow travellers had said that the manager looked like a typical Mui person, but Yona didn't know what a typical Mui person looked like. The manager's skin was dark, but lighter than the other Belle Époque employees. His frame was much larger, too, and he often had an overbearing look. Like right now.

'The days after the chaos unfolds,' he said. 'That's when the living and the dead are divided once more.'

He quickly returned to a soft, benevolent expression. Relaxing his face, he continued in a low voice.

'What will save Mui more than anything is the real disaster that comes after the disaster. That part is your role, Yona Ko.'

Fate can be determined by a single moment. Maybe the manager's offer was an opportunity for Yona. Yona fiddled with her glass of alcohol. Of course, this could be a trap. But if it were Kim here, if Kim was in this situation right now, maybe he would have liked what was going on.

The manager and the writer filled their glasses completely, and Yona filled hers halfway. The three drinks crashed in mid-air. A single sip of whisky warmed Yona's insides.

5

The Mannequin Island

—

IT WAS EARLY IN THE OFF-SEASON, and there were no guests at the resort. Weather wasn't good between July and November, so tourists' footsteps disappeared from Mui during those months. Disasters didn't distinguish between the dry season and the wet season, but things like precipitation, temperature and humidity mattered to the disaster tourist. The off-season had started just as Yona's Jungle group arrived in Mui.

Each morning began with a clear sky. As the day deepened into afternoon, heavy rain would fall, but at night, humidity and noise on the island vanished. Yona stood on her balcony, staring down at the sea and up at the sky. It looked like you could scratch at it with your fingernails, and if you did a layer would peel off, and then another identical layer would appear underneath. Wasn't there a saying that only thirsty people dig wells? Mui was a thirsty island planning a huge scam to survive, creating holes out of nothing.

The island's situation resembled Yona's, although it was significantly more dire.

Things had changed in the few days since Yona had agreed to take on a role here. Her previously unresolved problems were now dealt with quickly. The first evidence of this came the next day, when a resort employee went to Ho Chi Minh City airport and brought back Yona's suitcase. Of course, Yona still didn't have her passport or wallet, but when she was reunited with her belongings, she began to relax.

Yona wrote a contract to formalise the situation. By July, she would deliver the complete programme itinerary to the manager, and beginning in August, all business between Mui and Jungle would operate through Yona Ko. That was the gist of the contract. Yona decided she would remain in Mui until the first Sunday of August, but to stay here for more than a week, she needed authorisation. Yona had to secure written permission for a longer stay. Paul, it seemed, would grant her that permission.

'It's because Paul pays taxes to Mui,' the manager said. As Paul had invested in Mui, it had gained an enormous amount of authority. The manager told Yona that he'd already applied for her residence permit, and it should arrive within a week. Yona's first assignment was to explore the entirety of Mui, for research. The manager assigned an employee to help her with the task. It was the man Yona had given two dollars to: Luck.

The manager offered them a car, but Yona forcefully declined. It seemed less stressful to ride Luck's old motorcycle. Yona had forgotten until just now, but Luck had transported her back to the resort on this vehicle, after she'd witnessed the truck accident and right before she fainted. The motorcycle's paint was peeling off in fish-like scales.

'I couldn't properly say hello the other day,' Yona said bashfully. 'Your name is Luck, right?'

'Yes – you remember me.'

'Do you know my name?'

Luck shook his head.

'It's Yona Ko. I remember seeing this, too – the spelling here is wrong.'

Luck's face seemed to redden slightly. There was a Korean word on the body of Luck's motorcycle, containing a letter that wasn't exactly a ㅊ but also wasn't *not* a ㅊ. A long vertical line stuck out from the top of the letter. Yona gestured the correct spelling with her finger.

'This says *kyeongchuk* – celebration,' she explained. 'Do you know what that means?'

'Is it something good?' Luck asked.

'Yeah, it is. Luck, your English is really good. I guess you know some Korean, too, right?'

'I'm learning. I only know a little.'

The manager described the route to Luck. Today's plan was to visit the volcano and hot springs. As soon as she was handed the itinerary, Yona lightly crumpled the piece of paper in her hand.

'I'll decide where we go,' she told Luck.

They began on the road that circled the island. Mui formed a long oval shape, longer from top to bottom than east to west. The road went around the entire island, but it didn't always hug the coast. In some areas, the road veered inward, far from the water, so certain areas of interest weren't visible. After circumnavigating Mui once, Yona and Luck left the paved road and turned on to a dirt one.

As they drove, Yona couldn't help but lean against Luck. She was reminded of what the man who'd taken her to Phan Thiet a few days ago had said. That you could tell the relationship between people riding a motorcycle together based on their posture. The man had told her that she was sitting like luggage; not a partner, lover or friend. She still didn't know what it meant to sit like luggage, but she could tell that right now, Luck had tensed up just like her. When they drove on to bumpy terrain, he told Yona to grab him tightly, but as soon as Yona put her hands on his shoulders, he stiffened a little. On the paved road, Yona had been grabbing his shirt tails instead.

As she clung to Luck, Yona realised that backs have faces. How strange that a single movement could make her, and someone else, feel so awkward. Yona had chosen this old motorcycle over a comfortable car because she'd thought for some reason that the motorcycle would be easier. Its tracks were lighter than a car's, and with the motorcycle, the manager couldn't intervene. If Yona had picked the car, maybe the manager would have come along, too. But now Luck's back was making Yona feel strange.

They reached the Unda house from Yona's homestay, shrouded in quiet. Yona didn't see the schoolhouse boat, nor the child who'd floated by in the plastic basin. The whole area stood at a standstill, like it was a movie set that operated only during business hours.

But she did see one familiar child. A boy by the well. The well was familiar, too, of course, but it lay unused. The handwritten sign that the college student had stuck in the ground after the Jungle group finished their project, and the saplings that the teacher's daughter had planted, were already gone. A perfectly fitted top covered the well, and to the side, a heap of earth and sand was piled up, like someone had decided to plug the hole again.

The child noticed Yona and stopped moving for a moment. Yona saw his expression briefly change to one of contempt before he was overcome with the sadness of someone who'd lost his mother. 'Mum?' he asked Yona. Earlier, his face and this question had made Yona want to hug the boy, but now she had the opposite reaction. Yona stepped backwards. When Luck came closer, the child disappeared.

After the boy vanished, an old dog looked up at Yona and then lowered his head. When she'd been on the Jungle tour, even dogs had seemed like incarnations of disaster, but this dog just looked normal. The hammock the child had been lying in was now a fishnet, catching nothing but empty wind. The dog under the hammock fell asleep. Above, the blue fabric fluttered comfortably. At a glance, the hammock looked like a blue cloak coming up from behind the dog's back.

'I met a woman named Nam when I was here,' Yona said to Luck. 'Do you know her, by any chance?'

'Nam is a common name. And Mui people only come to the homestay houses when there are tourists.'

'Women with the name Nam are Unda, right?'

Luck smiled slightly.

'Unda and Kanu don't really mean anything,' he said.

'Why?'

Luck thought for a moment, then answered with the following.

'Because now there's a bigger divide.'

Luck told Yona he was going to show her what a real Mui stilt house looked like so she could understand the division. Yona wonder what 'real' meant in this case. The motorcycle hurried onwards.

After they passed the red sand desert and approached the ocean, countless houses on stilts rose up from the water. The number of them dwarfed the small set of homes Yona had visited in the white sand desert. The homestay village there was approved but fake, and these homes were unapproved but real. One third of Mui's residents lived here.

'About three hundred people live here,' Luck explained, 'but they leave in the dry season and then come back in the rainy season. They set their houses on boats and move them.'

'Why did Mui ignore the real houses and make fake ones instead? Tourists don't even know this place exists.'

'This is an unlicensed area. These people aren't really allowed in Mui.'

'Are they Unda? Or Kanu?'

'No one pays attention to that now. These people are just poor, so they can't pay taxes.'

A sign that read 'crocodile caution zone' rose up from the water, teetering to one side. Five-metre-long crocodiles had once made appearances here, but they'd disappeared; only the people in their unlicensed stilt houses remained. They trickled away during dry weather and returned to the sea for the rainy season. Problems arose when they returned. Paul wouldn't give them residence permits. Even before Paul, they'd never got along with the government. Eventually, a set of unspoken rules had formed. Tourists stayed in Mui between Monday night and Saturday morning. From Monday at 8 p.m. until Saturday at 11 a.m., people living here weren't allowed to go to the 'tourist' areas. The rainy season was the off-season, but even though Mui had no visitors then, the people here still weren't allowed to pass through tourist destinations.

Later, back at the resort, when Yona told the manager where she'd been, he warned her about the crocodiles. 'In the rainy season, they come up to shore and it's a real headache. Most animals don't hunt if they're full, but crocodiles are an exception. Crocodiles bite everything that moves, even if their bellies are full. Once they've started to bite, they won't let go unless you poke them in the eye.'

'It's best not to go there,' he added. 'It's dangerous.' An enormous map of Mui lay unfolded on his desk. Yona had never seen a map of the entire island, but because this one detailed only a few features, it wasn't very user-friendly. The manager circled five places in red pen and told Yona to include them in the travel programme. Among the five were the attractions Yona considered top targets for removal: the volcano and the hot springs.

'The volcano isn't even really a volcano,' she protested. 'It just puts a stain on the entire trip. Is there a reason I need to include it?'

'You're the expert, Yona Ko, so your opinion matters, but you should think about how locals might feel.'

The manager put two lumps of French sugar in Yona's coffee.

'We consider volcanoes to be very sacred here,' he said.

'But the customers are outsiders, and from a foreign perspective, the volcano doesn't look like a volcano.'

Yona had thrown herself into planning the Mui programme schedule, so there wasn't room for the volcano unless she put it at the end of the itinerary. The manager's insistence upon the volcano had nothing to do with its holiness or how locals felt. Yona didn't learn this until later, when Luck surreptitiously told her, but Paul had bought up most of the land around the volcano.

'Is Paul somehow connected to the red sand desert, too?' Yona asked.

'There's a plot of U-shaped land surrounding that desert, and you can tell immediately that it belongs to Paul. It's the only place over there that's fertile. They don't let just anyone into that area.'

Yona remembered that the land by the 'crocodile caution zone' had also curved into a U shape. The land's fruitfulness brought the residents there into constant conflict with Paul, because Paul wanted the fertile land they were living on. The area was like a pocket of sumptuous fat, butting up against acres of lean meat. After the planned disaster on the first Sunday of August, this land Paul had purchased would be covered with the golden eggs of tourist cash. Yona eventually decided to acquiesce to the manager's demands and included the volcano in her itinerary. The more she was pushed around like this, the more it felt like she was being used to fulfil the interests of a few people rather than help Mui as a whole. This made her uncomfortable, but was there any job where you weren't pushed around? Now Yona understood why the manager had wanted to plan the travel programme beforehand, why he'd entrusted this work to her, and the weight on her mind lightened. Even if only a few were benefiting from this, it seemed like she would be one of them, so she kept her mouth shut.

Outside, thunder boomed uproariously, but they couldn't hear it in the manager's office. Yona suggested that they construct a restaurant or hotel next to the volcano's crater. Staying at a site of potential danger for a long period of time would heighten visitors' nerves, and make the volcano a more worthwhile attraction. The manager worried that the volcano wasn't completely dormant, but soon he too was imagining the potential appeal of placing a tourist attraction right next to the crater.

Apart from going to breakfast, the writer spent entire days alone in his bungalow, where he did nothing but work. Breakfast was the only time Yona ran into him. Every morning, he would show up, with eyes bloodshot and hair dishevelled, and order a single egg. Yona's only opportunities to speak Korean came when the writer was around. Because he was Korean, he reminded Yona of the day-to-day life she'd left behind – of her entire past, beginning with Jungle. The writer called to mind everyday life. Maybe he felt the same about Yona, because he often used the phrases 'us Koreans' and 'in our country' when speaking with her.

'Yona, do you know when disasters become issues?' he asked.

'Huh?'

'Not all disasters catch your eye. The ones that become real issues are distinct. They typically have the following three traits. First, the intensity has to be over a certain threshold, depending on the scale used to measure that specific type of disaster. If it's an earthquake, above 6.0 on the Richter scale. If it's a volcano, above 3 on the Volcanic Explosivity Index. Even if the story's all over the headlines, that might not be enough. The disaster has to be on a certain scale for busy people to take the time to sympathise and pay attention. The world is overrun with stimulation, so that's just how it is. Interest has to be sincere. Secondly, the disaster has to take place somewhere new. Frequently repeated names are no fun. They're expected. Even if a disaster isn't serious, people pay attention when headlines mention an exotic place.

Think about it. You see a collapsing road on TV – but if all the road signs and traffic signals are covered with familiar words and letters, or, let's say, the types of people on screen and the clothing they're wearing are all too familiar, doesn't it get a bit tiresome? Empathy can fade too. But if a new, devastated environment appears before you, previously apathetic cells in your body buzz with energy until you feel fresh pain. The last thing is most important: the story. When people browse through newspapers after a disaster, they don't just want to see how terrible the wreckage is. They're also looking for an emotionally resonant story, sprouting up from the pain – it's easy to forget that.'

The writer seemed intoxicated by his own words. His gestures grew as broad as his sentences were long. His hands repeatedly spun around him as he spoke, surging upwards and tangling together, until he knocked a fork off the table. The writer expected a resort employee to pick up the fork for him, but when no one did, and no one brought him a new fork, he got upset.

'It's always like this here!' he exclaimed. 'There's no oversight, no oversight at all.'

The writer brought a fork over from the next table. The room always had several tables set with utensils, but no one except Yona and the writer ever ate there.

When preparing a disaster programme, you had to take pains to ensure that no matter how you divided up the trip, each part of it would still induce empathy and sorrow. Powerful images caught people's eyes. Images controlled the essence of disaster, especially when you encountered the destruction indirectly. If you compared several disasters that had occurred at similar times and with similar intensity, you realised that the scale of harm wasn't necessarily proportional to donations or public interest. Some ravaged cities appeared in newspapers as a few short lines of text before being forgotten, while others received extended interest and generous donations. Photos that recorded these cities' destruction, and the human-interest stories that surrounded those photos, sparked attention. When readers saw people like themselves, they felt bad for them and wanted to help. To control the public's emotions, you just had to reveal how much the victims' lives were devastated; in the best cases, those ruined lives induced empathy. The writer was currently fleshing out every possible fact about Mui's future victims. He didn't need to be very creative, considering how eagerly people read stories like this, but he did have to decide who would die. The writer's notebook contained dozens of pre-determined casualties. A mother and son, an engaged couple, an elderly husband and wife who'd lived in harmony their entire lives, a family whose newborn baby was spared, a teacher who died saving her students, parents whose young child survived, an old dog that dashed into the chaos to save its owners.

Yona had initially been told that they were going to use 'mannequins' to portray the casualties, but it turned out that the mannequins weren't actual mannequins. 'Mannequin' was just the name; in reality, they were bodies. Six months earlier, Paul had set up a scheme where families in Mui could earn a fee by donating the bodies of their loved ones for medical research after they'd died. The bodies were called 'mannequins', stored in the local crematorium's deep-freezer. The freezer currently contained about sixty bodies, which were all being preserved for the first Sunday of August.

The mannequins would play the leading roles in August's field day. That first Sunday of August, they would be thrown into the sinkholes. The writer was considering setting fire to the hellish pits afterwards to destroy trails of evidence. No matter how you looked at it, the plan had no relation whatsoever to 'medical research', but at this stage, Yona was beyond objecting.

The mannequins needed names and stories, and the writer's job was to create them. He endowed the bodies with stories. People who didn't know each other, or did but weren't very close, or had some other sort of connection, became co-workers and relatives and lovers. They lay silently in the crematorium's freezer, awaiting combustion. The writer said that the mannequin method was used often when fabricating emotional stories.

'You might say I'm killing a man twice, but I see this as more of a resurrection.'

'Have most people on Mui donated bodies like this?' Yona asked.

'When they've been killed in traffic accidents, yes. Although traffic accidents are the most common cause of death here ...'

'Traffic accidents?'

'The law in Mui doesn't take vehicular manslaughter seriously. It's more of a headache if the pedestrian is gravely injured. Then the perpetrator is responsible for the victim's life. If the victim has a family, the person who hit him or her has to support the family members, too. Because the settlement money for a fatality is a little bit lighter, most people try and pay the fee for manslaughter.'

Yona closed her eyes as she remembered the truck that had intentionally bulldozed the accordion man. She felt nauseous.

'So they kill people?'

'Most of the vehicles on Mui are trucks, so they can easily run over the victim and drive away. I was astonished, too, when I first learned this, but, well – in Korea, people sacrifice each other to save money, too, don't they?'

A honking sound came from outside, and Yona dropped her fork. She quickly picked it up, but she didn't have enough of an appetite to warrant bringing over a clean one, so she stood up from her seat.

Casualties weren't the only things being prepared. There were injured and unharmed witnesses, too. Locals would be paid to act out a performance of survival. During the first rehearsal session, the actors were handed lines for characters with names like Man 1, 2 and 3, and Woman 1, 2 and 3. They began to read the lines aloud.

'All of a sudden, I saw cracks in the floor and the

walls. I couldn't shut the door or windows all the way, either. They'd seemed like they didn't fit into their frames for a while, actually.'

'I kept seeing cracks in the ground that looked like the age rings on trees. I thought it was, well, strange. But I didn't expect the ground to collapse like this.'

'I heard a terrible boom and went outside to see everything crumbling. A hole opened up beneath my feet. My older sister got sucked inside, but I couldn't do anything. It all happened in an instant.'

Already, they were practising the lines they would need for post-disaster interviews. The payment for saying a line or two equalled six months of an average Mui salary. Lots of people volunteered. The mannequins readied themselves to be casualties, and the living readied themselves to survive.

Yona walked out to the beach. The horizon wrapped around Belle Époque like a wall. At first, this atmospheric border had calmed Yona, but now it seemed constraining. Yona said to herself that this place was nothing more than a large theatre. An empty theatre on the ocean, floating like a buoy, never sinking and never stable.

Yona had seen the crematorium before, from Luck's 'celebration' motorcycle. Despite being a facility that burned bodies, smoke hadn't come out of it for the past six months. Uniformed employees bustled in and out of the building, making it look more like a large supermarket than a crematorium. They all wore yellow vests and hats bearing Paul's logo. They moved busily within their assigned zones, like they were receiving new inventory. Several bodies seemed to have just come in; the workers carried cargo covered with blankets, transporting them here and there. It was hard to believe that the objects being moved before Yona's eyes were once living beings. They looked like merchandise.

The back of Yona's neck grew chilly, and soon thick rain fell from the sky. Luck grabbed a parasol lying in front of the crematorium's entrance and held it up like an umbrella. It was large enough to cover both Yona and Luck, and underneath it everything quieted.

'Luck, do you know what I'm doing in Mui?' Yona asked.

'You're reorganising the travel programme, right?'

'I'm worried I'll leave something out, so if you know of any potential attractions, feel free to speak up. You know, if you've got information about Mui that's useful for a disaster trip itinerary.'

She felt wary calling her project a 'disaster trip'. Luck was a Mui resident – maybe the phrase made him uncomfortable. But his response surprised Yona.

'Honestly, I don't even know what kind of disasters Mui has experienced. Before tourists started visiting, there wasn't much on the island. We had nothing at all, and nothing's not exactly a disaster.'

Yona didn't know what to say. Maybe only outsiders thought Mui was poor. Perhaps it was arrogant for foreigners to describe Mui as a disaster zone. Soon the streaks of rain tailed off, and after several last droplets hit the parasol as noisily as a flock of birds in flight, the rain stopped.

The sun lowered in the crimson sky. Palm trees absorbed the last sunlight of the day. They resembled the totem poles that marked the entrance to a traditional Korean village. There seemed to be faces in the bark: Halloween pumpkins, with eyes, noses and mouths alight. When Luck asked where to go next, Yona replied with her own question: 'Where's the place in Mui that you're most afraid of?'

Luck singled out one spot. Night came quickly on the island, and as everything came to a halt, the day's last destination appeared. The place was covered with enormous animal-like trees. Luck told Yona that trees possessed so much strength, they had to be fed growth suppressants. They were called 'strangler fig trees', and they could crush solid rocks between their wild branches. The broken rocks at the base of their trunks looked like cut-off heads.

'I've seen this kind of tree before,' Yona said. 'They grow at Angkor Wat, too. Apparently they can even eat up buildings.'

Yona looked up at the trees as she spoke. Luck tapped one of them.

'This one's a little different,' he said. 'It's unique. There's a legend surrounding it. When I was young, my mum told me that if I stood in front of this tree, I would see ghosts. So whenever I caused trouble, she threatened to hang me upside down from its branches.'

'What kind of trouble did you cause?'

'Nothing big – just hitting, pushing, fighting with my younger siblings. That kind of thing. My mother would always say, "I'm going to hang you two upside down from that tree." Whenever she said that, the fight stopped.'

'Are there still kids afraid of being hung from this tree?'

'It's a little different now. No one talks about ghosts here any more. Now they say you'll face your fears. According to the new legend, when you stand in front of the tree in the middle of the night, the thing you fear most appears.'

Yona and Luck walked in a circle around the tree. Even if the two of them stretched out their arms as wide as they could, they wouldn't reach around the thick trunk.

'What about you – what did you see?'

'When I was younger, I saw my mum. It was really strange, because my mum was alive, so she wasn't a ghost. But I saw her whenever I stood in front of the tree. It makes sense if you believe in today's legend, because the person I feared most at the time *was* my mum. Then, after my dad died, I started seeing him instead. If you think of my dad as a ghost, it makes sense that I saw him, but the truth is, that isn't why he appeared. I started to fear him after his death.'

'You must have thought of your dad a lot after he died.'

'Yeah. Even though I couldn't see him, it always felt like he was looking down at me, which I found a little scary.'

'Can you still see your dad?'

Luck looked at the tree. A flock of birds flew

overhead, causing the tree's leaves to shake noisily. Yona stepped in front of Luck.

'Shall we go now?' she asked. 'It's pretty dark.'

When Luck walked ahead of Yona on the way back, she stepped in front of him.

'I'm a little scared. Can I walk in front? I get nervous when no one is behind me.'

Luck slowed his steps. With Luck trailing her like a shadow, Yona asked, 'How old are you?'

'Twenty-three.'

The answer came from behind her back.

'How old do you think I am?'

'Twenty-three.'

'You're lying.'

'Well, then, how old are you?'

'Thirty-three ...'

Yona felt like she really was twenty-three again. As if the last ten years of her life had been erased. Night overtook the sun's remaining energy, and the black silhouette of the palm tree in front of them looked like an animal, its long, flexible body shaking, its hair spiky and skin gleaming. They kept walking.

Yona's Mui programme was the most exciting itinerary she'd come up with during her ten years at Jungle. It was extraordinary: she'd even included a one-night camping trip in the desert, where travellers stood below strangler fig trees and looked through telescopes at the sinkholes. Maybe the combination of disasters past and present made the trip so thrilling. This programme did have one weak point: it didn't fit into any of Jungle's disaster categories. People might call the sinkholes a natural disaster, but they weren't really natural; maybe others would say the collapse was due to human error, but it wasn't an error, either. Yona knew that the trip's success depended on the intentional fabrication of all of it never being discovered.

Only three people knew the entirety of the plan. The manager, the writer and Yona. But if you counted the people digging the holes – the ones who could speak both directly and indirectly about preparations for the forthcoming incident – there were more like several hundred. Even so, the manager was confident that as long as the writer and Yona kept their mouths shut, no one would find out about the future disaster, because the other people involved were only partially complicit. There was a specialised system in place: the people digging holes didn't know what the holes would be used for, and the people putting bodies in the crematorium freezers only knew that they had to put bodies in freezers. The truck drivers only knew their daily destination and arrival time. Those who would play survivors memorised their lines for future interviews like their lives depended on it. Everyone's assignments fell under projects with different names.

Yona agreed with the manager. This was work. Whenever she heard the writer talking about the script, she felt as if she was reading a sad book or watching a sad movie. The situation still seemed formless enough that she couldn't believe it was actually approaching.

What felt more real was the fact that her residence permit had not yet arrived. The manager told her that Paul was sometimes delayed during busy periods, so not to worry, but the assurance clouded Yona with anxiety.

'If the permit doesn't arrive, what happens?'

Yona had already spent almost two weeks in Mui, and with the field day only seven days away, she couldn't tell what a residence permit was actually for. Hadn't she been able to stay here even without one? The most important thing, the contract stating that this travel programme would operate only through Yona, had already been signed. And she'd already received the down payment, hadn't she? Yona was doubtful that Paul could actually exercise any authority over her.

'It's a formality,' the manager said, 'but we've never had an outsider who stayed longer than one week. You could say the permits are a kind of rule.'

'So right now I'm staying illegally?'

'I said it's a formality – don't worry about it. The permit will be here soon. More importantly, how is the programme coming along? Show me what you've done so far.'

Yona said that she'd just finished initial research. She would need to investigate more before coming up with detailed plans. In reality, Yona was needlessly stalling. She wanted to make sure that she had her timing right, too, like she was playing a card game. The manager was nice, but not particularly trustworthy. In several ways, he reminded her of Kim. Yona planned to delay turning in the itinerary as long as possible, without letting the manager push her around.

She had a second reason for the delay. Every morning, Yona travelled around Mui on Luck's motorcycle. These excursions meant more to her than the research. From a motorcycle, you could see another side of Mui. The desert wasn't a desert, it was an enormous, gentle animal at rest. Its sandy winds no longer stung her. Most of all, Yona wanted to know more about her companion, Luck. When she looked at Mui through Luck's eyes, it became a different place. Yona and Luck took frequent walks, teaching each other their native languages.

Luck knew a lot of stories. Things he had heard, things he had seen, things he had experienced. Mui was filled with empty alleys. The road and buildings had crumbled, or residents had moved out. Luck and Yona slowly walked down the abandoned streets. At one point, Luck stopped in front of a green gate.

'This was Chori's house,' he said. 'Everyone who lived here has moved away. Chori died three years ago, when he was eight. That was during Mui's tourism boom. Visitors came in waves, and like most of the kids, Chori went out and worked in the tourist areas. His determination made him a hard worker, and he earned money carrying people's luggage on his back during desert tours. He worked all day, even when he wasn't feeling well.'

Eventually, a pile of tourists' luggage fell on hardworking Chori and crushed him. It was a pointless death. On his last day, Chori had carried sixty kilograms – an easy load compared to the burden of being a poor child on Mui. The load that crushed Chori consisted of a pressure cooker, a grill and propane gas: gear for cooking chicken ginseng soup and frying pork belly in the middle of the desert. Chori collapsed, and the guide apologised for the subsequently delayed schedule. Chori died after the travellers left.

The stories continued, following Yona and Luck as they walked, taking larger steps than they did, threatening to overtake them. One day three years ago, a fisherman who lived in one of these houses had gone out to the coast for work, only to come home soon after looking grim. He'd been told he wasn't allowed to fish there any more. Now that a resort had opened, only tourists could enjoy the area. Around the same time, a boy who made the most pitiful expression when he cried was suddenly 'selected' to work at the tourist homestay village. The child cried day after day, and tourists aimed their cameras at him. As he grew older, the tears he had produced so easily started to dry up. And so he was, of course, thrown out.

Luck began to talk about a house painter with a forty-inch waistline and the woman he loved. Because the painter's forty-inch stomach stuck out so much, it was hard for him to paint things below his waist, so he and his partner always worked together. The painter painted the upper parts of walls and the woman painted the areas out of his reach and below his waist. The two had to be together to complete a wall. They were together when they died, too, because a wall they were painting collapsed. As the wall fell down and crushed them, the woman stared at the man and the man stared at the woman. Their lives were over before they could close their eyes. And that's how they, along with the house, expired.

This was the story of Luck's parents. The entire town had collapsed; some survived, but Luck's parents died inside the house where they were working. Luck remembered the story better than he remembered his parents' faces. The death scene was like a reel of film, worn out from being played too many times. Luck could retell it calmly. The home still existed, in crumbled fragments before them. It looked like a stage: it no longer had a roof, and one wall was overtaken by a gaping hole. Construction of the red sand desert tower had caused the sudden collapse. When the tower was first erected, nearby desert homes had crumbled en masse for some reason that no one understood, and this home was one of them: overtaken by heaps of dark red earth. Yona followed Luck into the house. The sandy winds followed.

One side of Mui was being turned into desert, and the other side was being turned into city. Urban and rural, growing larger simultaneously. But when you stood in the middle of the desert, none of this meant anything. It just seemed to extend endlessly, and every part of it was still. Intermittent cacti marked the land like warning lights. Occasionally the wheels of passing vehicles kicked up dust, or desert breezes blew.

The desert didn't cover all of Mui, but desert sands carried by the wind mixed with the air that everyone on the island breathed. You'd find sand on the coast where fish were caught every evening, and over all the island's roads. It found its way under sofas and beds in family homes. The desert was the centre of Mui. And in that centre, a whirlpool had begun to spin.

Yona thought back to the script, now so familiar to her, for the events of the first Sunday of August.

At 8.11 a.m., the first hole opens as the land below suddenly begins to sink. Earth is swallowed up, decorations and prizes for Mui's field day are sucked in. People preparing for the events, and a wheelbarrow that was parked above the sinkhole, fall too. At 8.15, the second hole opens, and the workers above pour into it like grains of sand. The alarm begins to sound. Within a minute, countless people are swallowed up by the hole. In between these sentences describing sinkhole one and sinkhole two, other characters appear, like full stops or commas being stamped on to a page. These people play the important role of connecting the sentences, mediating actions. Some of them give the starting signal, others plunge into the holes, and still others drive cars into the openings; some people sound the alarm, some snap photos and some die.

Yona still couldn't tell the difference between what she'd read and what would actually occur. When she thought about the script, she felt dizzy. Later in the day, as she looked down from the tower's observation point, the idea of a tragedy striking this place seemed as remote as an old legend. Down below, daily life was continuing as normal.

But when she descended the spiral staircase and stuck her feet in the sloshing sand at the tower's base, it all hit her, and the forthcoming disaster seemed close enough to touch. Reality was coming, and Yona was standing in its path.

Yona struggled to sleep that night. She felt worried when she went to bed, and she was still anxious when she woke up, but the sunrise improved her mood a little. The people of Mui needed tourists. Jungle needed tourists, and Yona needed tourists. As long as this plan succeeded, Yona would promptly return to her original job at Jungle, and maybe she'd even rise up to Kim's level, or be assigned a position where Kim couldn't bother her. While the sun shone overhead, those hopeful thoughts twirled about Yona's head.

But sometimes even before dusk, she began to hear stories. A crocodile who'd trespassed on the resort's beach and was run over by a truck. This travel programme wasn't bringing as many benefits to Mui residents as the manager had boasted it would, or even as many as Yona had expected. It seemed to be doing the opposite. The manager had convinced people who didn't care about tourism to construct a resort. After construction was complete and tourists began to descend upon Mui, the entire island bustled with activity. But only at the beginning; as time passed, unforeseen problems rose to the surface. Some residents had hoped to get richer when the island became a tourist destination, but nothing about their living standards improved; only restrictions increased. Mui's most beautiful beach was limited to resort guests. No one else could walk on the shore without permission, and swimming and fishing had to occur in specified areas. If an outsider came to Mui and spent five thousand dollars on his or her holiday, only one per cent of the money would trickle down to people here. Four- and five-year-olds became merchants who went around hawking home-made bracelets and flutes. That was the only change. But now, even tourism had lulled. Yona doubted that a tourism revival would solve Mui's problems.

Yona could now draw a proper Mui map. The Mui that Yona had seen over the six days and five nights of her Jungle tour covered only part of the island. The real Mui cast a shadow three or four times larger than the Jungle one. Both Muis existed one after the other in photos on Yona's camera, but an invisible line divided them. The real tragedy, though, hadn't been photographed at all. The tragedy facing Mui wasn't the past or the future: it was the present. That couldn't be captured in a photo. Until now, Yona had never thought about this kind of disaster.

The last photo on Yona's camera roll was a portrait of Luck. She'd taken it in the desert. The image wasn't focused, but Yona didn't delete it. Luck's expression seemed to be moving slightly beneath the screen. Yona scrutinised it for a long time.

Yona's residence permit still hadn't arrived, but she was clearly no longer an outsider. If she were, she wouldn't be seeing trucks so often. Yellow trucks bearing Paul's logo drove by her with particular frequency.

Sometimes the yellow trucks delivered mail, other times they transported goods, and sometimes they just caused accidents. Their drivers wore yellow vests and hats, like the employees at the crematorium. At one point, Yona overheard a conversation between two people getting out of a yellow truck. The conversation stuck with her because it was so normal.

'It would be nice if we didn't have so much overtime,' one worker said, 'but then again, when I'm not working, I get nervous.'

'We've got to keep our feet on the ground. Like fallen leaves, soaked with rain and stuck to the pavement. We can't let ourselves fly away, even when the wind is blowing.'

'Fallen leaves soaked with rain? That's a nice image. But the trees around here don't have leaves.'

After the two men got in their truck and sat in the driver's seat and passenger seat, the yellow vehicle darted forward at full speed. That night, Yona heard that there had been two traffic accidents on the ring road near the resort. Whenever a crash happened, people just sighed and said, 'Another traffic accident?'

Kim got in touch, coincidentally, right as Yona was finishing up the new travel programme. He said that the guide, Lou, had contacted him. Kim knew all about Yona's ordeal, but only now did he ask if she was okay, like this was the first time he'd heard about her situation.

'Anyway, we're not going to be able to renew Mui's contract,' he said. 'Just finish what you're doing as soon as possible and then come back. What the heck are you doing there, anyway?' Kim's voice sounded a little tired.

'I haven't been replaced, have I?' Yona asked jokingly, but the question made Kim lose his temper.

'How many times do I have to tell you before you understand? The company's in chaos right now. It's all because of the fouls. Come back quick. You must have done more than rest during your break. Surely you've come up with some new ideas.'

Kim's phone call felt like a threat, and it reminded Yona of the reason she'd initially resolved to stay here. After the call, she vowed not to let all she had achieved with the new itinerary be taken from her. Finally, the programme package was given a name.

Mui Sunday.

A five-night, seven-day trip.

6

Adrift

—

YONA HAD NEVER SWUM in an ocean. She only knew
the sanitised waters of swimming pools. But now, she
pulled off her T-shirt and waded into the night sea.
Luck stood in front of her. He stared silently at Yona's
thick dark hair, and she moved towards him. Luck felt
awkward staring continuously at Yona, so he closed
his eyes.

'Your eyes are closed,' Yona said.

Enveloped by darkness, Yona continued to speak
and began to touch Luck's eyelids.

'Does that mean you're one of the bungalows?
Should I not come in?'

Yona's wet fingers traversed Luck's eyelids and
touched his cheeks and lips.

'Is that really what it means?'

Luck didn't say anything.

'Why are your eyes closed?'

Finally Luck replied. 'If I open them, I'm afraid
you'll look too big.'

The moment he raised his eyelids, Yona kissed them. Very briefly, and then she moved away. Next, Luck's lips touched Yona's neck for a moment. They spent a while together, eyes neither open nor closed, unable to let their lips meet for long. Yona wanted to hug Luck's wet body a little more forcefully. Their breath came out rough and laboured, but the waves hid everything. The two were frozen, and nothing but the waves moved.

Only after Yona returned to her bungalow, after he saw the light in her room turn off, could Luck leave. Yona sat in her room in darkness, thinking about how their bodies had connected, the moment her weight had shifted almost entirely on to Luck. Maybe Luck was still sitting quietly nearby. Yona turned the lights on again. She pressed the button on her remote and turned on the eyelid signal light. Luck knocked on the door. That night, crashing waves drowned out all conversations inside this seaside resort. The waves came and went like the rhythm of a lullaby.

The curtains in Yona's bungalow remained closed through the morning. They slept deeply, the bungalow's eyelids closed, like it would be all right if they stayed here forever. Only at lunchtime did Yona feel appropriately hungry.

'Yona, I'm surprised by you,' the writer said sarcastically when they ran into each other at lunch. 'That guy's getting fired,' he continued.

Yona was only half listening as she walked out of the lobby.

'Toying with a Korean woman? We can't just let that go.'

'What are you trying to say?' Yona demanded.

'I saw everything. I saw it, I'm telling you. I stumbled across you guys on the beach last night. I was going to intervene, but it seemed like both parties were making a one-time mistake, so I decided to let it go. It needs to stop here.'

'I wasn't being coerced.'

'Then was money exchanged? Is this the guy's part-time job?'

'Is it a problem for us to be together as a couple?'

'A couple?'

'A woman from Seoul and a Mui man. There's no rule limiting our interactions to small talk, is there? Nights in Mui have been pretty boring, but now I've found a lover to pass the hours with. Spinning it that way would make our relationship look better in your screenplay, right?'

The writer made an expression of surprise. He fanned himself with one of his documents.

'I guess the screenplay's been spilled, then,' he said seriously. 'There's no way to keep things secret on this stupid island with your idiot lover.'

'Junmo, you didn't have to try and deceive me,' Yona joked. 'I didn't know I would be part of your script.'

The writer looked wide-eyed at Yona.

'There was no need to specifically tell you,' he insisted in earnest. 'I wanted to include a relationship story, but the higher-ups kept sticking their noses in my plans, so now I only have a few remaining characters without determined parts. I had to give this role to you. I wouldn't have done this if you were going to get hurt, would I? And I noticed that you and Luck were already spending a lot of time together anyway. If this screenplay is made public later, you'll basically be the protagonist. You're going to become a heroine.'

Yona thought about it. She'd just finished putting the Mui programme together, and now she was going to be immortalised as its creator in a screenplay. Looking at it that way, the script didn't seem like such a bad thing.

'Since everything's happening according to your script, Junmo, we won't face any problems, will we?'

'There is one potential issue. Sometimes, when you're acting, it becomes hard to distinguish between reality and theatre. That's what's happened to you – it's why you fell in love with Luck. I'm still going to include the romance between you two in the screenplay, but I wish you'd chosen someone better. Why *him*, of all people?'

The manager called Yona and the writer into his office, interrupting the conversation. He could barely hide his nerves. Last night, a magnitude 8.0 earthquake had occurred nearby. The earthquake's aftershocks didn't reach Mui, but considering how the manager was acting, they might as well have. His anxiety had to do with the disaster recovery programme he'd hoped to win for Mui. Now the island nearby which had been badly affected by the earthquake would become a strong candidate for it instead.

'They benefited from another recovery programme

only three years ago. If they're selected again this time, all our work is going to go down the drain.'

The disaster was arousing a sense of competition in Mui. When the manager heard that damage from the earthquake included more than two hundred casualties, he couldn't sit still. He unfolded and refolded his map several times, repeatedly asking Yona and the writer if plans were progressing smoothly. Only the plan for the first Sunday of August could save the manager from his anxiety. They began to double-check details, but talk of work overlapped with talk of news, and eventually news won out. It was hard to keep talking about their outlandish performance when faced with their neighbours' actual suffering.

The manager turned off the TV and opened a bottle of whisky. Outside, another bout of torrential rain was falling. The elongated chandelier hanging from the ceiling wobbled rhythmically, like a cradle. The yellow light had a blackish tint to it, and its regular motion, along with the alcohol, made everyone feel tipsy. Yona sat underneath the chandelier, and the manager and the writer sat across the table from her. The manager looked apprehensive, and the writer who had been chattering away grew quieter as alcohol coursed through his body. Strangely, Yona felt at ease. The earthquake that had occurred across the ocean seemed like a clear-cut truth. Mui, by contrast, amounted to nothing more than an unintelligible shadow of reality. Within that shadow, Yona found herself saying the following: 'We shouldn't let this project get out of control.'

'I think it's time you stopped drinking,' the manager said as he cleared away Yona's glass.

'Think about it, Yona. Some people will die because of the sinkhole, but others will live because of it. And a lot more people will live than die.'

The sinkholes were like a lifeboat, he said. If you wanted to make things fair in an emergency, no one would be allowed to sit in a lifeboat while others drowned. Didn't Yona want some people to survive? Like conspirators carrying out a grand plot, they'd decided to sacrifice the minority for the majority. No different from cutting off the sprouts on a potato, or removing a bullet from wounded flesh: they were giving something up for the sake of what would remain. But who would be sacrificed?

People become brave and upstanding versions of themselves when remembering past disasters. But things are different when the disaster is happening. Witnesses don't see the disaster for what it is, or even if they do, they look on idly, or sometimes exploit the situation. The sinkholes occurring now weren't on the other side of the desert. They were somewhere unseeable, somewhere inside Yona.

In her dreams, Yona replayed the truck accident she'd witnessed. She didn't want to see the driver or the victim's faces, but the dream forced her to lift her head until she couldn't help but look forwards – at the criminal, or maybe the body. The dream always ended right before she caught a glimpse of the face.

Despite her work's smooth progress, an ever-present feeling of guilt surrounded Yona. She kept forgetting that the Mui Luck had introduced her to and the Mui she was currently slashing to pieces were the same place. During her time with Luck, Yona had grown cautious about everything on the island. She could free herself from this confusion when she was with him. That afternoon, he was taking Yona to the mangrove forest.

'It's a healing forest,' he said.

'I didn't realise it was so big.'

'It just looks narrow at the entrance – inside, it's a different world.'

They got on Luck's boat and floated deep into the woodland. This place was the only part of Mui that Paul's trucks couldn't access. Trees crowded the swampy expanse, and the wet forest floor kept cars from driving across. The only thing that could pass through the forest was a single, narrow boat. Beneath the trees, Yona and Luck spent the afternoon in conversation. They embraced carefully, like movement would cause them to be eaten up by time.

That evening, after Yona returned to the bungalow and showered, someone knocked on her door.

The woman standing on the step had a hat pulled over her eyes. She seemed to have come in secret. Yona didn't recognise the visitor, but something about her was familiar. Yona let the woman inside her room. She held out a stack of paper: the writer's screenplay. Did this stranger know something that Yona didn't?

Yona tried to look at her face, but only her lips were visible under the hat. An unusual smell came from her body. Yona had a bad feeling about her. She pushed the stack of paper away.

'I'm sorry, but the screenplay is the writer's responsibility. It's not my job.'

The woman seemed to be scrutinising Yona's expression. Thankfully, the room was quite dark, and the murky indirect lighting masked Yona's appearance. Silence filled the room. The woman stared at Yona like she was drilling into her. Her eyes looked uneasy, and desperate.

'If it's not urgent, can we talk tomorrow?' Yona asked. 'I'm tired.'

As Yona turned away, the woman grabbed her elbow, snatching at her like the roots of the strangler fig tree.

'Have you not read the entire screenplay?' the woman asked urgently. 'Here, look at it.'

Yona stared at the woman, and for a second, she caught a glimpse of her eyes. Eyelids without a fold, brown irises. They filled with tears.

'You can't tell anyone that I'm here,' the woman pleaded. 'But I had to come.'

'What do you want to tell me?'

'If you read this script, you'll know: these plans aren't normal. We have to stop them before they happen,' the woman blurted out. 'Massacre – isn't that what you're doing?'

'Tell this to the manager,' Yona replied flatly.

'You need to know.'

'Well, I don't know who you are, so why should I listen to you?'

'It's a massacre. You're planning a massacre.'

In that moment, Yona hurled the first thing she could get her hands on. It was just a bedside cushion, but it felt like a rock. The cushion fell to the floor without hitting the woman. Yona let out a shriek, unable to hold back the anger welling up inside her. She hated this unwelcome guest.

'From what I know, people volunteered,' Yona said after she calmed down. 'They're compensated, the volunteer performers. This is between those volunteers and the people who hired them. There's nothing we can do.'

'We?'

'Me. There's nothing I can do.'

Yona looked at the woman, and the woman laughed scornfully.

'If you read the script,' she said, 'you'll understand. There are people who were unwittingly given roles even though they didn't apply. People who are carrying out this stupid performance that they don't actually want to be part of. Here: everyone assigned the parts from Crocodile 70 to Crocodile 450 is going to die for nothing. These crocodiles don't have lines. They're not even practising; they're just going to die. Most of the crocodiles, even if they're alive now, have been given roles where they have to die. Do you really not understand what this means?'

'They're crocodiles. What kind of lines would a crocodile have?'

'Don't you know who the crocodiles are? Haven't you figured it out what that word means?'

Yona turned away. Of course she knew the crocodiles the woman was talking about. The people who lived in the crocodile caution zone by the red sand desert, the people who set Paul on edge. The manager had repeatedly told Yona that the crocodile caution zone needed to be 'cleaned up'. Every rainy season, he said, the crocodiles came to shore and caused problems, and the baby crocodiles were increasing in number.

Yona recalled something else that the manager had told her. 'Mui isn't big enough to house these crocodiles, you know. They're dangerous.'

'Why are you saying these things to me?' she asked.

'You have to know. What the manager's plan is, how the massacre will occur. We need to stop it.'

'I don't know what's going to happen.'

'Listen to this line in the script: *There were about three hundred of them. People who lived here during the dry season and left during the rainy season. Mui was their home, and what happened is sad – it's horrible. I've seen the encampment from a distance several times. This is all unbelievable. I knew a really lovely boy who lived there.*'

'What are you doing?'

'That's one of the lines. Only after the crocodiles die are they treated like people. They're being sacrificed for this awful tragedy. Do you not recognise this part?'

'I don't know what you're talking about. Who's supposed to be saying that? And why should I trust you?'

'That's one of *my* lines. Now do you believe me?'

The crocodiles didn't have any lines. That was all Yona knew. She wasn't sure how they would be massacred. Honestly, she would rather not know.

'I'm sorry, but there's nothing I can do.'

When Yona said that, the woman shook her head.

'You can help,' she said.

'Please, just go.'

'It took bravery for me come here, Yona Ko,' the woman said from behind Yona's back. 'It pains me to think that I participated in the unfolding of this event. Of course, at the beginning I didn't realise it would be such a big deal. The hole in front of me now is larger than I expected, and it's growing out of control. I regret what I've done. But it's not too late for you to do something. I don't want you to regret doing nothing.'

Yona pushed the woman and they struggled with each other until Yona shoved her outside. Yona felt dizzy. She thought of Nam. And of the hole, bigger than planned and growing, unchecked.

The next morning, when Yona finally opened her eyes after failing to fall asleep all night, the ceiling fan looked several feet lower than before. She wanted to hurry up and go to breakfast, where all she had to worry about was how her eggs should be cooked. Recently, the writer had hardly been coming to meals. Yona ate alone, crossed the empty garden, and returned to her bungalow. Just as she was beginning to suspect that the woman's visit last night had been a dream, the script on the table caught her eye. Yona picked it up and threw it in the bin. Yona had never seen the final plans for the sinkhole. She knew about the initial outline, of course, but clearly the plans had extended way beyond that now. As her confusion grew, so did the number of things she didn't want to think about.

No one in the writer's script was being told to stab someone with a knife, or push them into a hole. The people being sacrificed, though, didn't know they would die. Ultimately, this event would bury hundreds of people in the holes. People who knew were staying silent about the future carnage. The woman was right: a massacre was being planned, but so cleverly that no one was directly responsible for it. Every part of the plans for Mui Sunday had been divided into the smallest possible components, so the workers making the sinkholes happen focused only on the assignments given to them. Yona was no different. She occasionally thought about the overall plot of this event, but those thoughts were always followed by the consolation, or perhaps excuse, that all she could do was plan the travel programme. If someone had ordered her to push people into the sinkholes, Yona would have said no and left instantly. But because her contribution wasn't direct, Yona stayed silent, and as she got more used to her position, she grew insensitive to the effects of her work.

But she dreamed often. The dreams brought Yona into a new realm. They were dreams about an almost-complete world, a world that would collapse immediately after construction finished. Where a man with a forty-inch waist and his partner worked together, each painting the places their hands could reach; where an old dog drowsed under a hammock; where a child practised crying for money; where an old motorcycle drove on roads that weren't really roads: that world.

The script was still in the bin. Yona wanted it to disappear, but eventually she fished it out. As she flipped through the pages, she came face to face with a story that she couldn't have imagined. A story whose last scene showed Luck's dead body in the first sinkhole, after Yona had returned to Korea. A last scene where Yona, without her lover, faced the sky and shrieked like she was being torn to pieces.

'All the relationships in my script are approaching their expiration dates. You didn't anticipate this? Why include a love story if it's not a tragedy?'

The writer sounded frustrated. He said that he'd never written a happy ending. No one who hired him expected a satisfying end. Yona grabbed him urgently.

'It's your screenplay – you can write it how you want. Do you want to kill Luck? No!'

'I couldn't hurt a fly. Does anyone wish to kill random people? But I'm an employed writer. This is a highly structured process, and my job is the script – nothing else.'

It was like a food chain: the manager stood behind the writer, and Paul lurked behind the manager.

'Yona,' the writer added, 'you're not free from this system, either. And haven't I been telling you from the beginning not to get too attached to Luck? You've got to stop caring about him now, see?'

Yona ran to the manager's office. If the manager was in charge of the writer, she needed to see the manager, and if Paul was in charge of the manager, she needed to see Paul. Then she could save Luck, she thought. If there was someone else behind Paul, who would it be? Who stood behind Paul, driving him? The sun slowly sank towards dusk, and the manager wasn't in his office.

In the distance, she saw the woman who'd come to her room last night. Yona couldn't read her expression, but the woman's presence felt like an added pressure. Yona returned to her bungalow and pulled the plans for the revised Jungle travel programme out from her drawers.

Yona had included the mangrove forest in her programme itinerary. The idea was to make the trip seem like an eco-tour as well as a disaster one. Luck knew more about the forest's ecosystem than anyone, a fact that she now indicated in the schedule by adding him into the itinerary as the mangrove forest tour guide.

'Luck? You mean the Luck who works at this resort?' the manager asked in surprise when Yona notified him about the unexpected addition. She explained that Luck's knowledge of Mui's old legends and natural features was vital to the success of this new Jungle trip.

'That guy has a very important role now, doesn't he ...' the manager mused. 'What is it you are really asking for?'

Yona lowered her head to keep him from seeing her face. Maybe, as manager, he could do something about the situation. 'Please, don't harm Luck,' she said. She didn't want Luck to die while she was safe in Korea; she didn't want that kind of ending.

The manager looked at Yona for a long time. His incredulous expression showed that he hadn't expected a request like this.

'The screenplay will have to be changed quite a bit,' he said. 'You won't mind?'

Yona nodded her head. Eight-one per cent of the world's natural disasters over the past ten years had been floods and typhoons, and the disasters that caused the most casualties were earthquakes. But to Yona, those had just become work. Now, she faced a greater disaster: her feelings. Yona felt uneasy, like her emotions were a landmine that could explode at any moment. She didn't want the manager to see how vulnerable she was. The manager was no different to manager Kim. She might as well still be back in the Jungle offices. Yona didn't have the freedom to do anything but nod in agreement.

* * *

It was the first week of August. The clock ticked closer and closer to Sunday, and Yona's chest constricted whenever she thought about it.

But at least she know knew that Luck was going to stay safe from this disaster. The manager said that he would send Luck to Vietnam on the day of the incident. When Yona thought about Luck surviving Mui Sunday, she could breathe again. It felt like a closed window, trapping stale air inside, had opened again. That evening she was going on one last tour of the island with Luck.

The drove out to the desert, and when they parked and started walking, Yona told Luck that her work was now finished. Their excursions around Mui by motorcycle could have ended ages ago, and Luck knew that they were just circling between the same places over and over again on this narrow island.

'Are you going home now?' Luck asked.

'Probably ...

'Shall we go together, Luck?' Yona asked. The words bounced out of her mouth before her brain could give permission. Of course, it was true that Yona wanted Luck to come with her. But he probably wouldn't be able to leave. They'd only spent three weeks together. If she went back to Korea with Luck, what would they do next? She was afraid. She stared up at the stars. Her question for Luck swirled in her ears, an echo in empty air.

The incomplete tower stood like a lighthouse above the desert. If you shone a flashlight down from the tower's peak, you couldn't see the sand below. Similarly, if you shot a flashlight up from the bottom, the light wouldn't reach the top. Luck spoke amid the endless dark.

'Scientists have filmed a video that records a brain thinking. Have you seen it?'

'Uh ...' Yona replied, puzzled.

'I've seen it. When someone begins to have a thought, a lot of changes occur inside the brain. The video captures that, and it looks exactly like a Christmas tree. The lights in the brain turn on and off, shining and then extinguishing. They twinkle.'

'Have you even seen a Christmas tree before? This is a tropical country.'

'What place doesn't have Christmas?' Luck asked, then smiled. 'Actually,' he continued, 'I only saw a Christmas tree in person after the resort was built. I've seen a lot more stars than I have trees. Now that I think about it, that video of a brain looked like the sky. White stars twinkling on a black background.'

Yona followed Luck's gaze towards the night sky. In the next moment, she began to cry as she listened to his unsteady voice.

'When I think about you after we part,' Luck said, 'my head is going to fill with those twinkling stars. Neither of us will be able to see them, but they'll definitely be shining.'

In the quiet, early hours of morning, Luck and Yona gazed up at a sky full of stars shooting in all different directions, as endless desert cactuses stood sentry around them. Luck looked at Yona with eyes full of tears. As the sun peeked over the horizon, he murmured that he'd miss her.

With that, another day in Mui began. That was the last time they saw each other.

Mui moved according to plan. Local fishermen were catching unexpected numbers of fish in their nets, as if nerves about the upcoming disaster were making the fish especially dozy. The sudden harvest surprised the fishermen, but they couldn't complain about it. Streets bustled with people pulling wheelbarrows full of the dead fish. Others could be seen hanging CCTV cameras on the desert tower and roads nearby, like they were decorating Christmas trees. Warning alarms appeared all over the place, like they were an animal infestation. Among generally smooth progress, some small problems occurred. Certain people disappeared. They died, or they left the island – no one knew exactly what had happened. Man 11, Woman 15 and Woman 16's roles were now unfilled. But the lack of a few characters wouldn't stop the gears from changing. Other Mui residents eventually filled the empty positions.

Yona had now witnessed several traffic accidents, and they weren't as shocking as at the beginning. But recently, the victims' faces had started to look a little more familiar. One of them belonged to the woman who had come to Yona's bungalow to ask about the crocodiles. Yona saw the woman being hit by a yellow truck, but she wasn't certain if it was a dream or if it was real. The woman had definitely disappeared. At some point, Yona stopped seeing her shadow wandering phantom-like around the resort.

'We just have to solve the crocodile problem,' the manager told Yona. 'If we throw bait at them, they'll all gather in the same place. We'll give them what they've always wanted – residence permits – and they won't be able to resist, will they?

This was exactly what the woman had wanted

to figure out: how the crocodiles would be driven towards their deaths.

The manager's words fitted into the big picture Yona was drawing in her mind. Yona tried to dull her feelings about the script, but occasionally the first Sunday of August appeared in her dreams. In the dreams, the crocodiles gathered two hours before the field day, overjoyed to have been given residence permits. Then the ground collapsed beneath their feet, opening the pits of hell.

It wasn't a dream, it was the future.

The only time that Yona felt untethered from this future was when she thought about Luck. Of course, this wasn't a perfect solution for her anxiety. When she thought about Luck, the crocodiles came to mind, too. Once Luck left for his business trip to Vietnam, running errands for the manager, Yona felt relieved. Luck wouldn't return until after everything was over. But her calm didn't last long. Mail arrived for Yona, filling another part of the puzzle in her mind, but it wasn't the residence permit she'd been waiting for. Inside the envelope bearing Paul's logo, a white image on a yellow background, was an unexpected sentence.

'You have been hired as Crocodile 75. You have no assigned lines. As compensation for your employment, three hundred dollars will be deposited into your bank account at the time of the performance.'

Yona checked the inside and outside of the envelope again. She couldn't find any instructions other than the sentence she'd just read. The addressee was clearly labelled 'Yona Ko'. Yona's heart beat quickly. What did this mean, Crocodile 75? Was it the same kind of role as Woman 1 or Woman 2 or Woman 3? Yona recalled what the woman had told her, the woman who'd visited her bungalow before disappearing: *everyone assigned the parts from Crocodile 70 to Crocodile 450 is going die for nothing. These crocodiles don't have lines. They're not even practising; they're just going to die.*

Clearly this envelope had been sent to Yona by mistake. Yona needed her residence permit, not an employment contract. And her life was worth more than three hundred dollars. Time was falling towards Yona like water.

Yona took the envelope outside and began to run. It was pouring with rain and she had nowhere to go, but she kept running. The people she passed as she ran tormented her; all of them seemed to be staring at her, repeating in unison, 'That woman is Crocodile 75.' She looked for the manager, but he wasn't in his office. The door to the writer's bungalow was also firmly shut. Several menacing bits of graffiti decorated his door. Disgruntled actors, dissatisfied with or afraid of their roles, must have already stopped by. The writer couldn't have been trying to dispose of Yona with this bit part. Didn't they share the same homeland? Someone had made a mistake. Yona already had a role: the role of Yona. Crocodile 75 – what did this mean? She called the phone number of the person in charge, written at the bottom of the envelope. The call connected quickly to her 'manager', Man 34, but he gave her an unremarkable answer.

'I was just directed to relay your role to you,' he said. 'That's my job. Why? I don't know. I'm not in charge there. Plans that big, I don't really ...'

No matter who Yona called, she got the same answer – from someone who was probably wearing a Paul hat and vest. 'I don't know what comes next. I only manage this part,' or 'I don't have control over that. I'm just in charge here,' or 'That's not my job; I'll connect you to the department in charge,' or 'Oh, the call got cut off? I'll connect you again.'

But eventually, the phone connected not to Paul but to Jungle's customer satisfaction centre.

'I'm waiting for my Mui residence permit,' Yona wanted to say. 'If you can't give me that, you can just send me back to Korea now. Why did I have to be hired as Crocodile 75? I never wanted this role.'

Instead, Yona said, 'I want to return to Korea.' On the other end of the line, she heard the computer keyboard clacking, quickly and cheerfully. It sounded like a card reader crudely spitting out a receipt. For some reason, the noise calmed Yona. The person on the other end spoke amid the clacking.

'You must have already read the terms,' she said, 'but you can't cancel a trip after it's started.'

'I don't need to be refunded. I don't need anything. Just arrange for me to return, please.'

'I'm not talking about a refund. You can't cancel a trip that's currently under way. You have to stay at your destination until the specified end date.'

'Why?'

'That's what the terms say.'

The computer noises coming from the Jungle office sounded both familiar and unfamiliar to Yona.

'If I'm sick, or a problem occurs, can't I just return to Korea?'

'Ma'am, you entered into a contract with different stipulations than a normal traveller. This is a business trip. You didn't pay for the travel costs. Since Jungle considers this a business trip, you can't suspend it in the middle.'

'Can you please connect me to Team Leader Kim? I want to talk to him directly.'

'He no longer works here.'

Yona's mind was fading to white. When she asked again, the woman repeated that Kim had left Jungle, and she wasn't authorised to tell her why. Yona hurriedly tried to call Lou, the guide from her trip. But Lou was in the middle of another programme, and the Jungle employee on the phone said Yona couldn't contact her. Yona had no one else to turn to. So she said into the receiver, 'Okay, I'll quit, too. I'll quit so I can finally do what I want.'

'According to the rules, it's only possible for you to quit in the middle of a business trip if you die.'

'Please.'

'I'll have to check if it's possible to quit in other situations. I'll get in touch when I find out.'

With that, the phone call ended. Yona knew the woman wouldn't check.

When she flopped on to her couch, she looked up at the ceiling fan. Its eight outstretched legs glared down at her. Yona pressed the 'do not disturb' button on her eyelid remote control. But the bungalow's eyelids didn't lower. No matter how many times she pressed on the remote control, it wouldn't do anything.

Yona stared out at the darkening sky. It looked like letters had been written in the dusk air. Maybe something was wrong with her eyes, or her mood was making her see things. She closed and opened her eyes repeatedly, until she saw that the hazy letters read backwards. If they really were letters, the intended reader wasn't Yona.

As she looked at the letters, flipped backwards and impossible to read, Yona thought about other things that had been chaotically turned around. Like the script's tragic romance between her and Luck. Had telling the manager about her feelings for Luck changed her fate? *When the manager asked if I'd mind him editing the screenplay, is this what he meant?* Yona brushed her arms, covered with goosebumps. The back of her neck grew chilly. The writer had said that Paul wanted a tragic love story. Yona had asked him and the manager not to kill Luck. *Does that mean I'm the person they've decided to kill?* Had they decided that they had to kill one of the two lovers? Count-less potential endings for Yona's relationship with Luck swirled inside her mind. She thought back to the website that told you the date of your death. Then, everything collapsed.

Yona's remaining lifespan was decreasing even now. That wasn't a surprise. But Crocodile 75? She thought she heard a knocking noise, and her chest sank. Yona went to the door.

'Luck?

'Luck?'

Even though she knew that Luck had gone on a trip, Yona hoped fervently that he was the one knocking. But when she opened the door, no one was there. Terrified, Yona began to run. She ran until she reached the strangler fig tree. There she saw something, hanging from the tree's branches. Dangling from the tree was the shoe she'd thrown out after the other two in her pair and a half were stolen. Yona didn't know why it was here now. Next, the child's sketchbook came into view. The drawings made by the teacher's daughter so long ago. Pages of the book turned over one by one in the wind. They looked like storyboards for an animated movie and Yona began to make out the pictures. They depicted things she'd seen or heard about on Mui. There was a sketch of the old dog that was always lying apathetically, here standing up and then running, following a smell, running into the sinkhole. Then it was dead. The dog ran into the hole, and after that, people gathered round and talked about what a faithful pet he had been.

Someone wearing a Paul hat that covered their face appeared and slammed the sketchbook shut. But when they lifted their head and turned to Yona, she saw her own lips under the hat, her own nose and her own eyes: familiar but unrecognisable. Slightly creased eyelids, brown irises, wet eyes. Yona froze in terror.

'Ask Paul,' said the figure. 'But Paul doesn't actually exist – didn't you know that?'

Yona's legs buckled, and she flopped to the ground. Her doppelganger began to run between the trees. If she didn't chase after herself, she'd be trapped, she thought. While Yona was running, black crabs crawled up from the sea in great numbers, and birds began to fill the sky. The palm trees shooting up like totem poles, the hidden forest beasts cried out. The forest was suddenly lit by two headlights, which charged forward and struck Yona. She collapsed, and when the headlights reversed and then accelerated again, Yona barely lifted her head. All she saw was yellow beams, glaring angrily at her. She glared back, but then the mass of iron crushed her slender body.

Time freezes. Two half-open windows appear before Yona; they let early morning light into the vehicle. Two eyelids, half-closed, or maybe half-open. Yona faces the window and stretches out her arm. Where did I go wrong? she wonders. Now she runs down a road with thick electrical lines stretched out above her, runs back to the starting point of her trip. She follows these electrical lines that look like tangles of hair, passing Mui's alleys, towards the sea, and now she's somehow going backwards down all the routes she traversed while in Mui. The moment that made everything go wrong: Yona fumbles around in her mind to find that point. But this is the culmination of countless, interconnected moments. This isn't my job, Yona mumbles resentfully, and then she encounters an inexplicable feeling of peace. Luck surviving instead of her – it's a blessing. Yona's body flows over the peaks and valleys of an emotion she hadn't believed she could feel until now: gratitude. Her eyes close halfway and then begin to pulsate. Do the pulsations mean that she is ready to die? Or are they an order: pretend this is not happening, because I'm still dreaming?

Yona forced her eyes open one last time, and then closed them. The sandy wind blew over her cheeks. That was how Crocodile 75 died.

7

Mui Sunday

–

THE WRITER WALKED OUT of the manager's office. Even at the resort, it was the only place with an internet connection. After staying up all night to finish the script and send it off, he wanted to check that his payment had been deposited. Today was Friday. The writer returned to his bungalow – passing dozens of ugly graffitied insults as he walked through the front door – closed his eyes, and immediately fell asleep. How long had it been since he'd slept so deeply? The two glasses of whisky he'd gulped down earlier helped him drift off into slumber.

On Saturday morning, the writer ate breakfast in the dining hall for the first time in a while, but he didn't see Yona. When he still hadn't run into her by early afternoon, he began to suspect that something was wrong. The eyelids on the front of Yona's bungalow were lowered, the curtains closed. The surrounding area was quiet, as if it had been frozen overnight; if you looked down, though, frantically moving creatures covered the ground. Fish had washed up onshore, and olive-coloured crabs crawled on to the sand in great numbers. The shore extended further out than usual, exposing the ocean floor. The sun shone down on an island already cleansed of last night's events.

Around sunset, the writer closed the curtains in his bungalow. He lowered the bungalow's eyelids and checked that he hadn't forgotten anything. A child who was familiar with the island's geography waited for him outside the gate. The writer had decided that on Sunday morning – when the sun rose in a few hours – he would escape on a private boat. If things had gone to plan, the boat would have had two passengers. But last night, the writer had learned, Yona died in a car crash. He didn't believe that Yona's death was an accident. He hadn't included her death in his script, and there were no plans to use Yona's body as a mannequin. The story was racing ahead of the writer, moving of its own accord. Yona had died, and when Luck found out he would be heartbroken. Paul seemed to have come up with an end to the tragic love story it desired, but without the writer's cooperation. He'd only written a scene where the two lovers parted in the desert.

In the quiet, early hours of morning, Luck and Yona gazed up at a sky full of stars shooting in all different directions, as endless desert cactuses stood sentry around them. Luck looked at Yona with eyes full of tears. As the sun peeked over the horizon, he murmured that he'd miss her.

In fact, the writer didn't know it, but Yona had veered off script. She and Luck had met once more after the intended farewell. He'd come to her bungalow before he left for Vietnam, and told her that he would wait for her in Ho Chi Minh City after he finished his work for the manager. That he'd see her off on her way home. That they wouldn't be apart for long.

After Luck made these promises to Yona and they kissed for what truly did seem like the last time, he ran off in a hurry. Yona called after him. She needed to tell him something, something other than confessions of love. She needed to tell him because of her love.

The writer couldn't know how much Yona had told Luck, or why she'd decided to reveal the plans for Mui Sunday. But he was certain that the person who'd divulged this secret was dead, and her death threatened him. He needed to leave the island as soon as possible.

* * *

The Sunday Mui had prepared for arrived. Man 1 loaded the correct number of airtight sacks on to each of the truck beds. He didn't know what they contained. He didn't really want to check. Not checking was probably better. Anyway, now that Woman 7 had delivered the cargo, all Man 1 had to do was hand it over to the drivers.

Man 12 boarded one of the five trucks. Each vehicle had a slightly different destination. Man 12 would be driving to the red sand desert's first hole. He had no idea what his truck carried in its bed. He was just happy to have work in the off-season. His job was to pour his cargo into Hole 1. He didn't know where Hole 1 was, but he'd been told that when he reached the desert's entrance, he'd be guided to the right spot. Two thirty in the morning. On the way to the red sand desert, the gleam of the white sand desert acted as streetlights. The moon shone with unusual intensity.

Man 16 drove behind Man 12. He was headed towards the red sand desert, too, but unlike Man 12, Man 16 felt deeply uncomfortable. He'd been paid too much. The compensation for this job transporting a load to a construction site was far larger than normal, and that made him uneasy. He didn't know what lay in his truck bed. He'd just climbed into the designated truck at the designated time, to carry the cargo to its destination. He wasn't calmed by the other trucks on the road headed in the same direction; instead, they heightened his unease. All sorts of thoughts ran through his head. Is a war breaking out? he wondered. Man 12 and Man 16 appeared to have the same destination. But then Man 12, who'd been ahead, suddenly disappeared off the road. His truck flew into the air before crashing down on top of Man 16's truck. The road stretched like a piece of toffee. An ear-shattering din erupted in all four directions. It was the alarm, sounding for the first time. Before Man 16 closed his eyes, he saw a waterfall of bodies cascading out of one of the truck's beds – maybe from Man 12's truck, maybe from his. In that moment, he noticed the expressions on the bodies' faces. Bodies of people he'd seen before, people he knew well, people he'd never met, fell like rocks. Several of them shattered his truck's windscreen and fell on top of him.

These two trucks, headed in the same direction, plummeted forwards together. The road they were driving over had diverged from its course. Back in the still-slumbering village, the warning alarm surprised Man 2. He looked at the clock on the wall. Three in the morning. The event wouldn't start for several hours. Man 2 had been trying to sleep, but couldn't. Nervous anxiety flooded his body.

Since the day he was assigned his role, Man 2 had wondered whether it was a curse or a gift to know the time of his death. His father had passed away after suffering from an illness his entire life. His mother had fallen sick soon after. The family tradition of dying from lack of medicine was passed from generation to generation. In a few hours, Man 2 might be buried in sand, but he didn't know if such a death was his true fate, or just the destiny he had decided for himself. He'd volunteered to become a casualty, but for a reason. Since he was doomed to an early death even if he didn't volunteer, maybe this was his fate. Once today's events began, four thousand dollars would be deposited into his bank account. That was far more money than the amount usually exchanged after a fatal car accident. Apparently, Man 2's role paid better than any of the others. With the money he'd earn today, the rest of his family could finally afford medicine when they were sick. The rest of his family was his mother and two children. His wife had emigrated to a foreign country years ago, and he hadn't heard from her since. If they were still together, maybe he would have made a different choice, but it was fruitless to imagine such things.

Man 2 began to shave. He needed acting skills for his part, because right before he died, he had to show himself to the CCTV camera near the tower. Because of that, this job felt more like a game than it did death. Man 2 had a lot on his mind. Pain shot through his chest. But the environment around him proved that his choice was the right one. He stopped shaving, and as he looked in the mirror, he remembered what he would have to do soon. He would drive his SUV into the first hole in the red sand desert. The hole was tremendously large and deep, so the people throwing themselves into it, especially those in large vehicles, had a high chance of dying. But maybe he'd live. If he had really good luck, he'd get his four thousand dollars and still survive. He'd been assigned lines to recite if he did make it. He practised them once more, and grew frustrated that he couldn't remember them precisely. It was an upsetting prospect, forgetting the lines he'd have to say if he survived.

This job was an opportunity. He wouldn't have even heard about it if he wasn't acquainted with Belle Époque's manager. He'd chosen to go down this path, so he didn't know why he felt resentful. The warning alarm in the distance continued to blare without stopping. The event was planned for 8 a.m. This was strange. His front door creaked open slightly, so Man 2 grabbed the handle to push it closed, but in vain. As the door opened, so did his eyes and nose and mouth and every orifice in his body. Earth, or maybe water, poured into the holes. The overpowering shriek of metal, or maybe waves, or maybe wind, swallowed his screams.

The screams repeated inside each home like an echo. As roofs caved in and floors collapsed, the houses were sucked over the horizon.

Woman 5 was vacuuming. A strange thing to be doing at three in the morning, but today was strange. Today, she had decided to let her comatose son go. Their last conversation had been four years ago, when he told her, 'I'm leaving,' as he set off for school, and she replied with, 'See you later!' She saw him next at the hospital, after he'd suffered a terrible accident and wouldn't wake up. She had been told to remove her son's respirator long ago. The hospital was requesting the unpaid balance, as it had done all it could. Today, the woman would hug her son before throwing both of them into the second hole. She'd been told that the moment they went into the sinkhole, money would be deposited into her bank account. The woman had written down the account of a friend who lived next door instead, to pay the overdue hospital bills after she and her son had died. She couldn't exactly grasp why she'd decided to vacuum at the moment she was about to end everything.

The dust bags usually bulged with debris, but today the vacuum cleaner didn't suck anything up. Woman 5 couldn't hear the sounds outside. As she turned the vacuum to its highest setting and wheeled it into the living room, the windows shattered into what looked like moonbeams and flew inside. For a moment, Woman 5 thought they were rays of light, but she couldn't see for much longer. The intruder was grey, with a hulking frame, and Woman 5's neck snapped easily in his presence. Only the vacuum cleaner survived, groaning through its wide-open mouth.

Man 4 heard the warning alarm and started his motorcycle. Strange: it was earlier than planned. He called the woman in charge, but she didn't answer. Woman 21: she must have been sleeping. He heard the warning alarm once again. He was supposed to be waiting for a truck. At around eight in the morning, he'd been told, the truck would arrive from some distant place, then the alarm would sound. His job was to flip a switch after the truck arrived and the alarm began to ring. But the sequence of events had come undone. The truck's tardiness and the unexpected alarm aroused Man 4's suspicions, but on an island where alarms never went off, the signal was clear. Man 4 had to flip the switch connected to Hole 2. He didn't exactly know what would happen when he flipped it. But for simply doing this so early in the morning, he would be compensated. Man 4 didn't know where Hole 2 was. All he had to do was flip the switch labelled number two, under the tower. It wasn't a difficult job. Something seemed a bit off, but he didn't need to indulge his curiosity.

Several people had already gathered beneath the tower. They wore similar expressions on their faces. The alarm rang for a third time, befuddling the group.

Should they interpret this as an order or a mistake? The alarm was supposed to go off at 8.11. They didn't trust such an early alarm, but as the sirens blared over an increasingly wide area, their bodies moved instinctively. They ran about in bewilderment, pulling ropes, pressing buttons, waiting for the designated time. Woman 8 stuck her head out from the top of the tower. She looked confused, too. When someone asked for a volunteer to go to the resort and find Woman 21, Man 20 and Man 4 raised their hands at the same time. Man 4 went to the resort, and Man 20 decided to stay where he was. They'd each been assigned a paid role, he figured, so they couldn't just leave the site. Even though he knew what was going to happen, Man 20's chest churned with disbelief. He felt like something was pressing down on his lower back and was seized with fear. Man 20 had volunteered because, like many others, he needed money more than he needed life. Some volunteers, it seemed, were playing less dangerous roles that didn't put their lives at risk. They must have been offered less money. Now Man 20 wanted to live. Death didn't seem as simple as he'd thought. He wanted to run away, to leave this place, to pretend that he was just going to the resort and would come back. He felt like he'd go crazy, standing at his future grave. Waiting.

After Man 4 left for the resort on his motorcycle, Man 20's legs buckled and he crumpled to the ground. Reading the expressions of the people around him only intensified his anxiety. Man 20's pocket contained knick-knacks that would identify him, as well as a photo of his wife to bolster his emotional backstory. The photo was fake. Woman 10, who played his wife, hadn't arrived yet. They were a tragic couple, killed three months after getting married. But Man 20 didn't actually know his supposed wife. Since being assigned the parts Man 20 and Woman 10, they'd spoken perhaps three times. He'd only been able to converse with her during rehearsal time at the volunteer meetings. Quickly, though, he had begun to think of Woman 10 as his real wife. Of course, this was just how he felt, but Man 20 wanted to hold Woman 10's hand and kiss her, to tell her stories and make promises to her. They had so many similarities: the environment they'd grown up in, the choice they'd made, their future stories.

Man 20 grew increasingly uneasy that Woman 10 hadn't arrived. As the alarm sounded again, someone moved forwards with the plan. Man 4 wasn't back from the resort, but someone activated the switch. Hole 1 began to collapse. At the same time, another sound came from the direction of Hole 2. The stalls and wheelbarrows stacked up in preparation – sets for a festival that would never happen – were washed away by the sand, spouting clouds of dust as they fell into the holes, throwing grains of sand as they struggled. Man 20 was supposed to run across the bog-like land between Hole 1 and Hole 2, land that would certainly collapse the moment he stepped on to it, but he couldn't lift his feet. Before he could decide what to do, his body began to run in what he thought was the direction opposite the disturbance, but the disturbance seemed to be coming from every direction.

Hole 1 was supposed to collapse, and then a bit later Hole 2 would collapse, but now the sky was falling, not the sinkholes. The tower crumbled in the direction he was running, its debris following him like a shadow. Or maybe this had happened: the desert palpitated, surging upwards before the tower's stones began to fall. The tower, the desert – everything – collapsed and tangled together.

A man standing at the top of the tower called out, saying that everything was okay, not to worry. He held a camera in his hands. His job was to take photos, but the camera got swept away, followed by his body. Everyone saw it. A man's body, pulled under the earth. The top part of the tower – which wasn't supposed to collapse – broke in two and fell into the sand, dissolving like salt.

Before Man 4's motorcycle reached the resort, before he'd made it out of the desert, he saw the tower and sand crumbling behind him. He couldn't tell up from down. His motorcycle soon veered off the road. Man 4 and his motorcycle didn't reach the resort, but wind and wave did. The resort was pretending to sleep; beneath the surface, it was a hive of activity. One bungalow was sending wire transfers, another was checking a CCTV camera, and in a third bungalow, people waited to be called to work. The alarm began to shriek, and the enormous wave that had already engulfed other parts of the island began to swallow bodies and houses and books. Letters from the books came off their pages, overwhelmed by the waves, and bounced in the water like fish.

The wave reached the manager's office, an uninvited, very powerful guest.

The manager raised his head and looked at this guest that was the size of a mountain, who'd used the entire ocean as a stepping stone, waiting in the sea before coming for the manager. It stretched its arms above him and then came crashing down. The manager ran down the emergency stairs. But the Earth was dancing. Thick tree roots appeared between the gaps in the ground, and the oldest of them coiled around the manager's ankle. Centuries of destruction occurred in a single second, and then all was quiet.

The wave embraced the trash island as it passed over the backbone of the desert and approached the village. Foreign trash, debris that had wandered across borders: it all flowed over Mui at three o'clock in the morning, and completely devastated the island in four minutes. Luckily, today was the first Sunday of August. Some people had erroneously believed that the day's events were occurring early, and they'd stuck to their roles faithfully. Others recognised that this wave had no relation to the plan, but that didn't help them survive.

At 8 a.m., the schedule disaster time, the sun rose over the horizon and revealed the aftermath. People lay on the desert and road and resort and shore, their eyes closed. There was no distinction between tribe or class. Tangled together, the people with closed eyes said nothing. Those who were still standing found the scene so unbearable they closed their eyes, too.

If you looked down at Mui from high above, you wouldn't be able to distinguish between the people and the trash. The resort, adjacent to the beach, had been hit hardest. Lines from the script that would never be performed fluttered in the wind and scattered around the resort. The wind blew forcefully, like it wanted to rub the words off the script, and the waves descended like they wanted to dissolve them.

Most of the survivors were discovered in the mangrove forest. After sunset the night before, those paying attention might have noticed the many crocodiles on the move. Houses on boats, houses with and without motors, houses that couldn't pay taxes, houses that couldn't live in Mui, and most importantly houses that would collapse at dawn if they didn't leave, crossing the sea one after another.

The houseboats had headed for the mangrove forest. That was Yona's idea. The forest could hide many things.

The morning after parting with Yona, Luck had run to the crocodile caution zone. He'd told the crocodiles that their new residence permits were a trap: if they wanted to live, on Saturday night, they would have to secretly move to the mangrove forest. Some crocodiles were suspicious of Luck. Others didn't believe him. But that was the best Luck could do.

Luck spent three days in Vietnam. He had accepted the abrupt travel assignment because he thought he would see Yona in Ho Chi Minh City, on her way back to Korea. Before leaving for the dock, he'd looked silently at the inside of his parents' crumbled home for the last time. On Saturday, some crocodiles migrated according to Luck's instruction, and others didn't. The houses that decided to move hid their bodies just above the water, like real crocodiles, and crossed the sea. They floated to the mangrove forest, where they survived the night. These people understood the danger of the resident permits and had fled in order to survive. But then the tsunami hit Mui, and everything changed. When the wave hit, the ancient trees of the mangrove forest wrapped their roots around the crocodiles to protect them, and as dawn came, the crocodiles realised they constituted the majority of the island's survivors. The survivors didn't have lines to remember. They didn't have lines to practise. They didn't have special alibis. They had no rehearsals and no compensation, but their stories flowed to the ocean like blood from a head wound.

Mangrove Forest

—

Northbound: High atmospheric pressure, cherry blossoms, news of deaths
Southbound: Strikes, debris, stories

STORIES.

News of the deaths had moved fast over the past week. Though initially high, interest in the deaths would inevitably dissipate quickly, especially once all the coffins had been carried away.

Before the news hit, most people had never heard of Mui. People were riveted by the story of the enormous tsunami, and the trash island it carried in its wake, which had smashed into Mui and then scattered into millions of pieces.

The trash island, larger than when it left Korea's southern coast, had departed from its expected course overnight and gone to Mui. People who'd been predicting the trash's path now began to retrace its movements. But they didn't see any human connection to the unexpected divergence. The only explanation was a powerful wind current formed by the Earth itself, an enormous flow that had pushed the trash island off kilter.

Diligent investigators discovered remnants of the sinkholes in the desert. The experts said the following: it looked like the tower's construction had overtaxed the foundation of the red sand desert, weakening the desert's stability. That, along with rain and drought, had caused the sinkholes. This was exactly the reaction the writer had expected. But thanks to the rage of an enormous tsunami, so massive that it had dwarfed the sinkholes, the writer wasn't around to witness the reactions. He was one of more than five hundred casualties. His drowned body had been discovered in front of an ashtray on Mui's dock. One last cigarette had likely divided life and death for him.

A surprisingly intact bundle of papers was found inside the writer's bag. Junmo Hwang's script caught people's attention because of its setting: Mui in August. The only difference between the script and reality was that one only had a sinkhole, and the other a tsunami too. People couldn't tell if the script was fiction or truth. A surprising record of survival and death, or a goosebump-inducing horror story.

The public interest focused on the Korean woman in the script, Yona Ko. A travel company employee, swept up and killed by disaster in a foreign land. When some of the woman's belongings were discovered in the demolished resort, curiosity grew. Her body still hadn't been found, but eager adventurers got hold of the script and began to look for its other characters.

At Jungle, increasing numbers of people called to ask about Yona. Most of the calls came from the press. Yona's replacement was too busy to remember the hazy face of her predecessor, and she didn't know how to answer these callers. The people on the other end of the line asked for personal information about Yona. But Yona's replacement knew nothing about her personal life. Clearly, Yona Ko hated leaving footprints behind. Co-workers with anecdotes about Yona offered up what they remembered, and a few of the stories were made public. In one, Yona lost her pair and a half of shoes; in another, she was ousted from a project she'd dedicated herself to. There was also the story where she lost her way at a travel destination, and another where she decided to extend her stay. No one would have remembered these anecdotes if Yona had survived, and some of the stories weren't even true.

Yona's replacement dealt with the Mui project speedily, like it was an obituary for someone at risk of fading from memory. She accessed Yona's emails and the plans for Yona's most ambitious programme yet were delivered to Seoul. Of course, the itinerary needed a little bit of editing. The volcano, hot springs and original sinkhole were all completely devastated, so Jungle had to fill the schedule with new attractions. One such attraction was the red sand desert's dismembered tower. Paul's tower had broken in two during the tsunami, and now an enormous tree was anchored between the fragments, like a bird's nest. A lot of strangler fig trees grew in the area. This one had wrapped its roots around the tower, creating a distressing scene. The tower was like the tree's new host. Jungle plastered its promotional materials with the image of these two intertwined structures.

Although the picture of the tower and the tree was shared widely as a depiction of Mui's disaster, disagreement bubbled up about whether Mui would tear the tower down or not. Mui received the disaster recovery funding that the manager had wanted, but no one could agree on the tower. Some said that it was a visual reminder of history, while others argued that it brought up painful memories and needed to be cleared away. Throughout several months of debates, the tower and tree continued an uneasy coexistence.

The new Jungle programme began before Mui was completely forgotten, while the two-piece tower still stood. Travellers arrived just as Mui entered the dry season, the best time to visit. They ventured to Mui for moral lessons and shock, volunteering and relief. On the third page of the information booklets they received, they saw the story and name of the travel programmer who'd met her end on a prior Jungle trip. Yona's name was enough of an advertisement that it couldn't be omitted. Yona's former guide, Lou, had written tributes not only for Yona, but also for Junmo Hwang.

In early morning, cameras appeared in the mangrove forest before the sun did. The tenacity of these trees that had withstood an enormous tsunami filled the travellers with wonder. The homes that had been transported there no longer migrated with the seasons and took root permanently in the forest. Someone carrying an enormous book sat down in front of one of the houses on stilts. The book shielded his face; the name Yona Ko was written on its cover. Travellers could walk behind this seated figure to see the contents of the book. A large picture of a camera covered one of the open pages, with a dollar sign on the other. Some tourists gave the man a dollar to take pictures of him.

Luck was one of the survivors. Because he'd been travelling, he had avoided the first Sunday of August. But when he returned to Mui and learned that Yona hadn't made it safely back to Korea, he collapsed. Tourists sometimes recognised Luck and came up to him in the hope of hearing his story. They wanted to take photos. Some pointed cameras or recorders without asking permission.

'The hem of a woman's skirt was fluttering in the wind. A red skirt. As she climbed the tower, each window she passed turned into a flickering traffic light. Once she reached the middle of the tower, the windows disappeared, and so did the lights. Dizziness overpowered me. That was our beginning.'

Jungmo Hwang had written these lines for Luck. Perhaps the tourists hoped that Luck would recite them, but he didn't say anything. Despite his silence, the visitors wouldn't leave Luck alone. They'd seen the photos recovered from Yona's camera. One had been an unfocused portrait of Luck, another a picture of

Luck and Yona reclining in a boat. Those two photos gave birth to the suspicion that Junmo Hwang's screenplay wasn't fiction. Luck couldn't stand to look at them.

'What kind of relationship did you have with Yona Ko?' people asked him. 'Were you lovers?'

'When was the last time you saw Yona before the incident?'

'Do you know where Yona's body might be?'

'According to that screenplay, you were Yona Ko's boyfriend, right?'

They attacked him with questions, rudely and transparently. But gradually, the questions became more infrequent, and increasingly vague. Eventually, when a group of tourists asked:

'Did you know Yona Ko?'

Luck simply answered no, and turned away.

Luck stood with his back to the group. Nothing but lies could save him.

He remembered the last words he'd heard Yona say. 'The crocodiles can hide in the forest. The mangrove forest.'

This sanctuary was now the only place for Yona to hide in death.

Luck walked towards the ocean, its waves creeping closer to land. Debris carried by the waves from Yona's mother country lay strewn across the beach. Luck could read some of the words on the scattered wrappers and bits of plastic, and couldn't read others. Next he headed deep into the mangrove forest. So deep that no one could follow him. Down a road so narrow that no camera shutters, no newspapers, no news of any kind could chase after him. As he walked, unseeable stars in Luck's head flickered on and off and on.

Behind him came the sound of the tower falling. The tree's roots had been wavering like a pendulum in the wind; if not for the instability, perhaps the tower and tree would have remained conjoined forever. But for safety reasons, it was decided to remove the tree from the tower, and then the tower, too, was plucked out of the earth. People had spent months arguing about the odd structure, but the tree was removed in less than ten minutes. As the tower and the tree came apart, several bodies that had been stuck between them fell like ripe fruits. Yona wasn't among them.

About the Translator

—

LIZZIE BUEHLER has translated *The Disaster Tourist* (Serpent's Tail) and *Table for One* (Columbia University Press), both by Yun Ko-eun. Her writing and short translations also appear in *Asymptote, Azalea, Litro,* the *Massachusetts Review* and *Translation Review*. Lizzie studied comparative literature at Princeton University and holds an MFA in Literary Translation from the University of Iowa.